Foreword

I read the book, "Don't Tell Mum I woik on the Rigs, She thinks I'm a Pianist in a Whorehouse" by Paul Carter, with enormous delight. It's entertaining and funny on most pages, and so it got me thinking. My own experiences in the mines were similar in many ways to this oil rig guy, with some (at least to my mind) equally amusing anecdotes. The major difference is that my mother doesn't think I am| pianist - she thinks I'm a penis.

So, here are some tales from the tunnels. Hopefully you'll find them as comical and interesting as I do, or maybe I really am just the prick my mother thinks I am.

I started my mining career at the tender age of 18 in the deep gold mines of the Transvaal in South Africa. At the time of writing (40 years later), I still work in the industry, sometimes. It's been a bunch of booze-ups, fights, and mining mishaps from the very beginning, set against the backdrop of the cultural miasma of mining locations all over the world. This book recalls some of the stories, the lies, and the exaggerations from those years. Some of which happened to me, some to other people, and some probably only occurred in the imagination of the storyteller from whom I heard them. What I can't remember accurately, I will of course make up and no doubt will come to believe in future years. While these tales for the most part do of course cover real-life events, they do represent my unreliable memoirs and should thus be taken with a bucket load of Siberian salt. My lawyer tells me that this is therefore a work of pure fiction, and no reference to any person living or dead is intended. Any resemblance to any living person is purely coincidental, but if you read this book and feel I have been an arsehole... I resemble that remark.

The book itself covers the three stages and ages of my life in the mines. First up is the story of how I descended into this profession, despite family pressure to take to the skies to fly fast jets in the Royal Air Force. Next are stories from underground where the more robust (for want of a better word) characters in life dwell, recounting the scrapes I got myself into while climbing the greasy management pole. Finally, the view from the bridge running small and medium sized mining businesses. The lonely feeling you get when you are the officer of the watch charting your ship through an ocean-load of super-tankers captained by lunatics. Tankers I said.

Enjoy.

Jack Shaft

Jackoshaft@gmail.com

Acknowledgements and Thanks

I am for ever grateful for the forbearance of my wife and loving family and the wonderfully supportive friends that this life has thrown up. There are so many to thank so I won't risk naming you, for to be sure, I will fail to remember some and then they will get away with pretending not to know me. Surely it is better that all of you to achieve this deniability. Thank you also to the participants in this story, for without you I wouldn't have a story to tell.

In this book I would be remiss if I didn't thank my editors. The intense editing work put in by Sam, Sharron, Melanie Scott, Oliver and Tony has been nothing short of miraculous, turning my leaden passive voice into what I hope is a dynamic active story, and my grammatical and spelling howlers into what is, I believe, now readable prose. I would also like to thank Vanessa Mendozzi for the brilliant cover design, and, Mark L for his sage marketing advice.

And finally, thanks for having me Mum and Dad.

JackoShaft@gmail.com

More details can be found on the "Its Been a Blast" facebook page.

First Edition

ISBN : 978-1-5272-6460-1

This book is a memoir. It reflects the author's present recollections of experiences over time. Many names and characteristics have been changed, some events have been compressed, and some dialogue has been recreated. My mother claims that while I describe myself as quite ugly, I am actually not that bad to look at. I've allowed some of these points to stand, because this is a book of memory, and memory has its own story to tell. I have done my best to tell these stories as reasonably truthfully as I can but given that the memory is at best flawed, this should be viewed as work of fiction. Names, characters, places, and incidents either are the products of the author's imagination or are used fictitiously. Any resemblance to actual persons, living or dead, businesses, companies, events, or locales is entirely coincidental.

It's Been a Blast

By

Jack Shaft

Era 1

The formative years, from adolescent to graduate

"May you have the hindsight to know where you've been, the foresight to know where you're going, and the insight to know when you've gone too far." – Traditional Irish Blessing

Chapter 1: In the Beginning

"Sometimes you only find out what you're supposed to be doing by doing the things you're not supposed to do." — Oprah Winfrey

I want to be a publican I tremulously wrote to my father who was labouring in the Nigerian bush. I was a 16-year-old about to embark upon my A-levels. I had been incarcerated eight years at boarding school by that time, and he had never written or communicated with me when I was away. My father was not a communicative man. At the beginning of each term, I waved goodbye to my family with two Cornish pasties in my pocket and a trunk full of ginger-nut biscuits, expected to return three months later a bit taller and a bit wiser. I only ever seemed to get taller.

I can only imagine that, on receipt of this news, my father spat out his metaphorical dummy, because the 20-page letter I received by return post used language somewhat more emotional than his usual style. Suffice it to say, he thought it was a really shit idea.

This led to some protracted navel-gazing angst on my part. My father, being in the RAF but on loan to the Nigerian Air Force at the time, had wanted me to become a jet pilot. I, on the other hand, thought that I was temperamentally unsuited to such a role, although some who know me now might disagree. Every jet pilot I had met was arrogant to the point of narcissism. So full of self-love that they probably got hard just looking at themselves in the mirror each morning. These guys were the big swinging dicks of the skies, and my bathroom was far too small a place in which to turn around in such a state. I certainly couldn't compete with them, being the skinny small-dicked runt that I was. Runt, I said.

So, writing off the idea of becoming a rocket jockey, I set about analysing the alternatives. I decided that the last thing I wanted to do was get stuck behind a desk. What I really sought was a life full of scrapes and adventures, in which I could be physically active.

I honed it down to three options: farmer, fisherman, or miner. I liked the idea of growing things to create value, and so I asked a farmer friend what it was like. It seems that if you have livestock you spend your whole life shovelling shit into one end, and then shovelling the shit that comes out the other end, with never a day off. He also advised me that life was hard on the farm and the wages were rock bottom. Clearly, unless born into a farming family or being fabulously wealthy – preferably both – farming was out of the question. I then thought about life at sea, but gallons of testosterone were coursing through my veins and I was hormonally driven towards horizontally jiving with the fairer sex. I had also discovered what was to become a lifelong love for craft beers. The thought of spending weeks away from women, beer, and song was about as appealing as jumping into a hot tub full of sick. So the idea of life on the open waves was also shelved fairly quickly. That left mining.

That summer, my father arranged a visit to the tin mines of the Jos Plateau in northern Nigeria with some miners that he had come across while drinking in a Kaduna bar. I recall the day with great fondness. During that first shift the crew had to work around an elephant-sized rock that was causing a nuisance in an open pit. As the day waned, we placed five sticks of powder and a detonator with a long ignitor fuse on the rock and heaped muddy clay on top of this small mound. We retired a supposedly safe distance to a rudimentary tin clad shelter. The shift supervisor lit the cord and walked nonchalantly back towards us. I watched the sparkling fire on the cord inching closer to the mud pile with mounting excitement. It reached the mud and fizzled out. The watchers, except me, casually yakked amongst themselves. Thirty seconds, which felt like an hour, ticked by.

A misfire I thought and was just about to turn away when the evening sky lit up with a glorious flash and a large plume of dust was thrown a hundred metres or more into the sky. Almost immediately a concussive thump hit me in the chest like an All-Black thumping himself during the haka. The land rumbled and shook as the evening sun was dimmed by a cloud of pulverized material. Golf ball sized rocks landed on our rudimentary shelter, hammering it like a demented hard rock drummer. It was like a Bonfire Night display with added danger and I was hooked. I loved the idea of creating something valuable out of dirt, dust and rocks. Dust to dough, ashes to tin. There followed a revolving round of parties and pubs. Big bangs didn't require much nous and were also a good deal of fun. In fact, I seemed ideally suited to it. I could visualise an active life full of laughs and joy, one which would lead to a contented retirement running a country pub, all the while regaling my loyal customers with tales from the depths, having quietly made my fortune.

Thus, in an act of defiance that was to define my entire working life, instead of taking to the air, I decided to do the opposite and go underground. Later that year, I discovered, quite by accident, that there were two scholarships to encourage young people like myself to embark upon a life as a mole. Clearly, the industry was running short of future victims. I applied and was to my immense surprise, invited up to London for two days of assessment. On checking in at the hotel the evening before the interviews, it rapidly became apparent to me that there were 29 other highly motivated candidates who had also been shortlisted. I got into conversations with a few of them and discovered that most were potential jet pilots with projected A-grade results. Clearly, there had been some sort of mix-up. My teachers had predicted that "Jack might pass if they only ask him what his name is, but we expect to see him in re-sits next year." I rapidly came to the conclusion that I was the outlier in this august body and therefore destined for early rejection.

I decided on the only course of action open to a bloke with my feebler mental capacities when faced with such unlikely potential for success. I set about getting royally drunk at the welcome dinner, smoking foot-long cigars and drinking industrial quantities of port. After all, why not make the most of a free piss-up while you can, for they would surely throw me out first thing in the morning? To my incredulity, and that of every single other person who attended the assessment, I lasted the full two days, and was one of the two candidates to receive a scholarship from the Mining Educational Association Trust (MEAT for short – the clue was clearly in the name) with the recommendation that I should go to the South African gold mines to get some real mining experience under my belt. It would appear that the criteria for candidates was not intellectual rigour, and upon just clearing the hurdle for my A-levels with a couple of passes, I set off for South Africa with two pasties in my pocket and a couple of packets of ginger nuts. My life in the tunnels was about to begin.

Chapter 2: The Deep Gold Mines of South Africa

"When you find yourself in a hole, the best advice is to stop digging." – *The Bankers' Magazine* (1964)

I landed at Jan Smuts Airport in Johannesburg (now renamed OR Tambo International) and worked my way through immigration to the arrivals hall. There was a quiet buzz in the reception area with people hugging and kissing hello. Standing motionless in the centre of this heaving mass of sentiment was a grizzly-looking fellow with a slightly vacant stare. Acting on the hunch that he was my reception party, I approached him and asked if he was waiting for someone. It came as no surprise when it turned out that he was waiting for me.

In an unlikely turn of events, my meeter and greeter, Herr Van de Merwe, proved to be an amusing character and storyteller. Not only was he missing a leg below the knee, but he was also missing a couple of fingers and had a glass eye that I discovered, he would regularly drop into a person's beer glass, thereby securing himself many a free drink from the disgusted recipient. The original eye and leg were blown off when a miner drilled into a misfire, an explosive charge that had failed to detonate during the blasting process. This occurred in a development end (known by the uninitiated as a tunnel) on one of the rare occasions when he was visiting a working area, but more on that later.

Quite why the company thought it was a good idea to send such an emissary, who was both maimed and darkly cynical, to pick up the new blood is one of the many imponderables of this life. Perhaps they had heard about my penchant for stag-do quantities of booze and cigars and didn't really want me. It backfired spectacularly. Van and I immediately found a common language, stopped off in the nearest bar, the Jolly Rogerer, for a few cool refreshers, quickly becoming muckers.

The South African gold mining industry nestles predominantly in the Witwatersrand Basin, south and west of Pretoria. The Kloof gold mine, where I was to work, was at the very heart of this old inland sea. The gold reefs found in this basin are generally less than two metres thick and extend to depths in excess of three kilometres below the surface, with approximate dips (the angle of inclination from horizontal) ranging between 20 and 35 degrees. However, it would be a while before I would be let loose in that playpen.

For the first few months, while incarcerated with a bunch of other ne'er-do-wells in a room euphemistically termed the Learner Official Training Centre, the mine indoctrinated me. We certainly didn't learn very much, and we were the least official group of trainee troglodytes it's been my duty to goof off with. This was the era of apartheid in South Africa, an appalling, ugly and disgusting regime in which white people lived completely separately, with the system preventing black people from achieving anything. This evil arrangement has thankfully long gone. Notably, the wisdom of a white miner in those days did not exceed his beauty. They even made me look passably intelligent.

The indoctrination included instructing and drilling in the regulations of the mining industry and being taught to speak Fanakalo, a creole language which is a chaotic mix of English, Afrikaans, Zulu, Xhosa and slang. Gunster and I, a cynically humorous German who had also breezed up at the mine at roughly the same time quickly renamed it "Funfuckalot", and had endless fun creating new words. "Lo fly machine ka lo nightshift" for a bed. "Columbussing" – when a white person pretends to discover something that has been known about for centuries by the indigenous folk. "Askhole" – someone who asks really stupid questions. We had quite a lot of need for that one. There were also some incredibly strange phrases in the textbook issued for our edification. My favourite was "Dij kamel im likimbat bo dat kanggaru irrahol," which literally translated means "The camel is licking that kangaroo's ear." Undoubtedly it has connotations, but I still have no idea what they are or when you might ever need such a phrase. Gunster and I became lifelong buddies during this year of experience.

As a brief aside, anybody who thinks the French have a sense of humour and the Germans don't, has got it completely wrong. After all, who else could sell the idea of sharing a currency with the Greeks and the Italians with a straight face. The French, meanwhile, suggest that someone has 'swallowed a clown' if that person is being funny. This tells you all you need to know about French humour. Whereas German humour is relatively sophisticated as the following Gunster joke illustrates...

The United Nations initiated a poll with the request, 'Please tell us your honest opinion about the lack of food in the rest of the world.' The poll was a total failure. The Russians didn't understand 'Please'. The Chinese didn't know what an 'opinion' was. The Europeans didn't know the word 'lack', while the Africans didn't know about 'food'. Finally, the Americans didn't know anything about the 'rest of the world'.

Oddly enough, Gunster's mum was French. Given his humorous outlook, I wondered if she had swallowed a clown.

The Learner Official Training Centre was an extension of chalk-and-talk teaching and was, bluntly put, torture. Fortunately, this deskbound torment didn't last, for there is only so long you can listen to some barely upright hominoid comrade fail to remember his two times table. In a fairly short timeframe, I found myself underground, shadowing real miners in order to achieve the two hundred 'dusty shifts' that would enable me to sit the blasting exam. That test at the end of the obligatory training and dust dosing was mostly a single choice answer test. It was like multiple choice, but there was only one choice. I just had to get my name right, tick the boxes and answer a couple of open questions to achieve a blasting ticket and become a miner. I didn't quite score a hundred percent though. My answer to the question, "What steps would you take if you saw a two centimetre blue flame on your miners' safety lamp?" of "Bloody long ones" was not seen in the comic light I had intended. Incidentally, the Davy lamp, invented by the renowned Cornish scientist Sir Humphrey Davy, gives the user a strong indication of methane gas levels by burning more brightly with a large blue halo on the flame. Apparently fucking off quickly was only fifty percent right. I scraped a pass.

On my first day as a certified miner, I made the cardinal sin of arriving at the shaft at five minutes past five in the morning. I was late for the five o'clock cage, the metal box suspended by a rope in the shaft that takes people and materials down the mine to different levels. The shaft mine captain approached and did a traffic light impression, going from orange to deep red and then green. From three millimetres in front of my nose, he bawled me out:

"Why are you late, Shaft? Did you need your beauty sleep? Is five o'clock too early for your delicate English constitution?"

"Sorrysirwonthappenagain," tumbled out.

"Where are you from, Shaft?"

"Er, England, sir."

"Did you miss the bit about your English constitution? I fucking know that, you shit-for-brained berk, where in England are you from?"

"Suffolk, sir."

"Suffolk. If I'd known you were from Suffolk I could have explained that we're not on a farm now. Did you milk the cow before you set off? Have you been out looking for the lost sheep of your dreams? Did you ride your tractor here? The fucking cage waits for no fucking one," he finished.

I was sent back to my flat with the admonition that if I was ever late again it would be cause for instant dismissal. Boet van Rensburg, a kindly hoist driver (a hoist is very large winch, which lifts and lowers the cages with people, materials or rocks in the shaft), took me to one side and told me not to worry, and that the captain's bark was worse than his bite. Boet was a solid Afrikaner with a beard like Father Christmas. He was considerate and helpful, which was a rarity in those hard days, and I really appreciated his fatherly guidance. He advised me to spend the rest of the day looking for a vehicle to get me to and from the shaft changing rooms on time. I did find a rust bucket in the local paper, an Alfa Giulia, which according to the ad was a good runner. This was partly true. You needed to be a good runner to own it, as the only way to start it was to park it on a hill and then bump it into life. It was barely better than a tractor, but it solved a whole heap of other problems. I called the clanking banger Julia the Giulia.

To say that Julia had challenges was an understatement. Her radiator didn't work properly, so I took great care when going uphill in the summer. While driving up inclines I'd have to pull over and shut the car down so she could cool off every ten minutes or so. Failure to do this would result in the release of copious volumes of steam from her front grille, which could be pretty disconcerting for nearby pedestrians.

Julia also had a leak in the driver's side door, which would leave a small pool of water where my feet were after any rain. This was especially bad in the winter on the frosty Highveld. On a cold morning, the water would freeze and create a mini ice-skating rink in the footwell, which added additional degrees of complexity for gear changes. I awarded myself ten points every time I didn't ride a red light.

There was also an ongoing challenge with the fuel tank. The issue was the pea-sized hole on the right side, which chewing gum only seemed to adhere to for a week at a time. I couldn't fill her more than halfway or she would leak fuel, and I had to take care to park her right-side tyres on the curb so that Julia leaned to the left. Otherwise she would leave her mark, male dog style, on the pavement below.

Despite her faults, I loved this car. She got me to work, the drive-in movies and the pub. She sometimes had to take a breather, it's true, but she only wheezed when she was really pushed to great effort.

Think about that old story of locking your girlfriend and your dog in the boot of your car for ten minutes and then testing who is most pleased to see you when you let them out. I call this comparison the 'yardstick of reciprocal love', and Julia was on a notch near the top of the pole, closer to the dog end. She chuffed along happily most of the time with low maintenance, huffing and puffing when excited, and was nearly always pleased to go out for a jaunt.

Chapter 3: A Miner

"Being stupid is like being dead... it's only painful for other people." – Ricky Gervais

On my second day, I arrived half an hour early in my splendid, newly acquired metal horse. I descended into the bowels of the earth where I was to lead a team of thirty labourers, given oodles of explosives and contracted to wrest gold-bearing ore from two miles down.

Here I ran into the one-eyed Van de Merwe again. He had the panel of ground just below me and was breaking all records for extraction. I couldn't work it out. I spent all day sweating my nuts off with my gang on the face, shovelling, marking, drilling, and yet every time I got back to the miners' crib station – the underground office and waiting room – Van was always sitting there, feet up, reading the paper, smoking his illegal pipe. He had covered the smoke detectors with a condom to conceal this heinous crime.

One of the time-critical activities was cleaning the blast from the previous day. The downward slope gradient of the ore bodies, or dip, was roughly thirty degrees, which is slightly less than the natural angle of repose of broken rock. The head height was just over a metre in our stopping panels. In essence, the working area for one person was like being in the dark inside a telephone box that has been leaned over onto a beer barrel, with the floor sprinkled with sharp stones and boulders that slip as you crawl around on them. The miner inside the box carried a heavy battery on a belt to power the lamp on his helmet, the light of which picked up the swirls of rock dust in the air that he breathed.

To look at it another way, the whole working stope panel was akin to a box of chocolates with the chocolates left in place, but the plastic retainer removed. The chocolates act as support for the lid, which has a rather large fat cat sitting on it. The weight of the cat results in the chocolates in the middle of the box being crushed flat so that the middle chocolates are only two millimetres high. The actual working areas are on one edge of the box, and this is where new chocolates are being wedged in to support the cat as the box gets larger, after each blast. Imagine now that this box has been expanded to belly-button height and covers the area of a football field. It has been tilted at a thirty-degree angle with rocks and rubble strewn all over the floor. It's completely dark, but as hot as the hottest day you have ever experienced and humid to the limit of human endurance. Every now and then, the cat jumps on and off the box, and when this happens, the lid flexes. This does happen in real-life stopes, and sometimes the roof, which we call a hanging wall, fails with tragic consequences for any miner in the vicinity. Makes those fishing and farming jobs look pretty sweet, doesn't it?

After a blast, the newly broken rock would need the assistance of shovels and water to move the rubble to the bottom of the panel – the lower end of the chocolate box. A miner would scrape this broken rock into a cousin jack, or loading chute, using a large metal bucket attached to a winch. The chute had a door on it, which was opened to load wagons that transported ore back to the shaft. This washing down and shovelling was hard work and needed a canoe crew of shovellers on their knees, all working in time and without pause.

Clearing away this muck quickly was critical to preparing for the next blast. I could see that Van's team always managed to get his muck cleared away twice or even three times faster than my team. There had to be some special method that I didn't know about. Maybe he was sending in an early crew, maybe he had more people on the task, maybe he was inspiring them with great leadership and oratory. It was certainly true in my limited experience that the South Africans loved a good storyteller. I settled on the latter as the obvious truth.

I decided to craft an inspirational speech to win loyalty, passion and effort from my team in my now fluent Fanakalo (translated here for the reader's edification), and the next day at the start of the shift I assembled my crew in the usual fashion at the miners' crib station. Standing on the wooden table I addressed the hushed team:

"Friends, miners, rock breakers, lend me your ears!

We come to dig rock, not to sit sleepily in the back blocks,

Let's come together as one and strain every sinew to win this gold from the bowels of the earth.

Let's stress and strain and leave no stone unturned in our quest for riches and wealth!"

A throaty deep sound resonated from the team. The word "Umbala" came rumbling back to me. I was onto a winner here. "Umbala" hadn't been on the Fanakalo course, or at least I didn't remember it, but it was clearly a term of utmost respect and endearment.

Thinking that it wasn't good to leave an expectant crowd gagging for more, I decided to give them another dose. What could possibly be wrong with yet more passionate words of inspiration and motivation?

"On this team, we fight for every square centimetre... On this team, we tear ourselves and everything around us to pieces for that centimetre... We claw with our fingernails for that centimetre... Because we know when we add up all those centimetres... that's going to make one 'more of a big bonus' for us all!"

The expectant crowd gave me an even louder "UMBALA! UMBALA!" I had really got the bit between my teeth now and, calling on recollections of Teddy Roosevelt, I delved into my old school memories and exclaimed in my most dulcet tones:

"The credit belongs to the man who is actually on the coalface, whose face is marred by dust and sweat and blood; who strives valiantly; who errs; who comes short again and again, because there is no effort without error and shortcoming; but who does actually strive to do the deeds; who knows great enthusiasms, the great devotions; who spends himself in a worthy cause; who at the best knows in the end the triumph of high achievement, and who at the worst, if he fails, at least fails while daring greatly. His place shall never be with those cold and timid souls who neither know victory nor defeat."

"UMBALA! UMBALA! UMBALA!" the crowd roared back.

I sent them off to work in the stope, smug and secure - in the self-satisfied, self-assured way that only a teenager can have - that I had inspired them to yet greater work effort and that we would all reap the reward of a massive payday.

This story does have a sobering ending, of course. That very weekend, visiting a local farmer and wandering around the cattle-fattening yards, I was admiring the plump, happy, lowing cows, meandering from one pen to the next, when the thoughtful farmer pointed down to the ground and warned me to, "Please be careful, and step around that pile of fresh Umbala..."

I still hadn't got to the bottom of Van's secret to super-production. One day, a few months later, I cunningly waited for him to set off to his working area from the miners' crib and quietly followed him, keeping well back in the darker area, my lamp on dim and pointed to the ground. He would see me if he looked in my direction, but I was not obviously there, and he didn't look back anyway. I settled into a comfortable spot in the worked-out area and turned off my lamp as I watched him setting out the work plan with his team. It was pretty much the same as mine, no special secret there. He barked instructions and tasks to his crew, organising their day's activities. Then, to my amazement, he lowered his voice to a sonorous, almost priest-like tone and a deathly hush came over his entire crew. "I am watching you with my evil eye," he intoned, and carefully placed his glass eye on a rock just back from the working face. His crew looked petrified and started rowing enthusiastically. Van then sloped off to the miners' crib. I kept my concealment for fifteen minutes more – nothing slowed down. The crew was clearly completely terrified and shovelled in perfect unison like an Oxford crew in a tight boat race. They never slacked off at all during my brief observation.

There was not much I could do in that regard, given my lack of glass eyes, but Van did get his comeuppance. Shortly after this epiphany, one of his crew tiptoed up behind his eye with a fourteen-pound hammer and shattered it into a million pieces. As pissed off as he was about this, his crew knew he couldn't identify the culprit. Whoever it was had made sure that the eye couldn't see him as he swooped in for the smash.

Chapter 4: Miners Sports

Miners will argue and fight, but let a shout come from
without, and see them unite. – Old Proverb

It didn't take too long to settle into the ebb and flow of mine
life. One interesting element of Kloof living was the Gold
Bar in Glenharvie, the local town. Strolling up to the Gold
Bar it was noticeable that the miners' womenfolk would sit
outside in their cars chatting, reading and knitting the night
away before collecting their husbands. No women came into
the miners' bar, and frankly, I didn't blame them. It was a
place of thick cigarette smoke where the wine list didn't
stretch as far as "white", surprisingly in such a noted wine-
producing country. In fact, if you didn't want a Lion and
Castle lager you were wasting your time. Now, from an
English beer drinker's perspective there isn't much to
recommend Lion and Castle, mass-produced beers that
tasted like beer line cleaning fluid that hadn't been properly
flushed between barrels, but they did have one saving grace.
It was cheap.

So, every Friday night, rough, hairy and angry
miner's whose lot in life was to beat and blast the earth into
submission would descend on the Gold Bar to smoke, drink
and brawl the night away. Some of them didn't have much
respect for puny tools like pickaxes, preferring to extract
their gold with a head butt – whether from an ore seam or
another patron's dentistry didn't matter to them. Their sole

aim seemed to be drowning or pummelling the remaining brain cell in their craniums. Invariably a brawl would start at ten o'clock. The patrons were so punctual in getting to the proper business of beating fifty shades of shit out each other that if you set your watch to ten o'clock on a Friday at the start of the brawl you wouldn't miss your five o'clock cage.

Being of a slightly less aggressive constitution, but still needing the occasional glass of the amber nectar, I quickly befriended a guy known as 'Gentle Pete'. Gentle Pete was enormous. The circumference of my rugby player's legs was much smaller than his gargantuan arms and Pete towered over the mine rugby team's second-row forwards. He was a giant and built like a brick shithouse. He was also the calmest, most easy-going, Labrador-charactered guy you were ever likely to meet. He liked a drink and, having once been a Manchester nightclub bouncer, he continued to practice his old craft on a Friday night by gently throwing errant miners down the Gold Bar steps to their grateful wives, who would dutifully pick up the crumpled, bloodied heaps and drive them home for tea. It always struck me as amazing that these same miners would turn up the next Friday to go through the same routine all over again. Pete was a useful guy to have on your side. He never got angry or emotional, indeed, he would sometimes be having the calmest of conversations with you, bang two heads together mid-sentence, and continue chatting as he heaved the dazed miners through the swing doors, all without blinking an eye or pausing for breath.

I once asked Pete, "Have you ever gotten angry?" He thought for a while and then said, "Once I was sorting out a massive brawl in the nightclub and some Yardi came up behind me and hit me with an iron bar. Then I got a bit irritated." I can only imagine the carnage. Nobody ever messed with me in the Gold Bar, of course.

Another minor incident occurred during my tenure as a miner in South Africa that first year. One of the miners tasks was to dispose of the old explosives which had passed their expiry date. The explosive we used at the time was dynamite, which is nitro-glycerine mixed with clay. Nitro-glycerine is a primary explosive: it's very easy to detonate. A useful property when you want to blow something up, less so when you want to store or transport it.

This is where the clay comes in. By mixing nitro-glycerine with clay, Alfred Nobel (yes, the man who, after reading a premature obituary of himself describing a "merchant of death", established a peace prize) created a desensitised secondary explosive – dynamite – that was less responsive to shock or vibration. It was harder to set off and safer to handle when working in a mine or ammunition factory. To set off dynamite you use a detonator with a small amount of primary explosive in a primer cartridge, which of course needs very careful handling.

Unfortunately, in secondary explosives, the nitro-glycerine doesn't stay in the clay indefinitely and over time it leaks out and degrades, becoming more sensitive until eventually your explosive store becomes a little more delicate as the nitro starts dripping from the boxes. As a general rule, the shift boss preferred it when you got rid of the dynamite before this happened.

The contract area I had inherited had tonnes of old explosives, built up over years by the hoarding miner who had worked the area before me. This hoarding had the advantage that any tool, part, or piece of equipment needed could be found stashed away there somewhere. Indeed, I fondly imagined finding some pit ponies and a cage full of canaries if I searched hard enough. Anyway, back to the old dripping dynamite; clearly this needed blowing up and I was the man for the job.

The rule for disposal in the handbook was to tie five sticks of dynamite round a primer cartridge with a detonator inside and then insert a delay fuse which you would initiate at the end of the shift before retreating to the shaft. To put my problem into context, explosives arrived at the working area in large cartons of twenty-five kilos of dynamite divided into sticks of about two hundred grams each – that is, each carton had a hundred and twenty-five sticks. For the first couple of weeks I dutifully followed the instructions, disposing of five sticks a day in the three old development ends under my control.

The rulebook method was getting through the old dynamite at just under one tonne per year. I had dozens of dripping boxes. Almost three tonnes of unstable explosive, and more was ageing every day. How long would it be before Van, tapping his pipe out, would set off the whole store? What if it didn't happen at the end of shift when the mine was empty? A more ambitious plan was in order.

I decided that if I wilfully misinterpreted the rule book, and tied five boxes around the detonator and primer, it would take a lot less time to dispose of the dangerous old stuff. I justified this by telling myself that the old boxes might be set off by the concussion of a regular blast anyway, and what could possibly go wrong? When it's gone, it's gone. I arranged my oversized bundles, lit the delays at the end of the shift and dutifully retreated.

Imagine my surprise the next morning when I was pulled to one side and dragged to the mine manager's office. Promotion already perhaps? On entering the room however, I realised that this wasn't going to be one of those good days. I could see steam hissing from the manager's bootlace holes, and cannonball-like blackheads about to explode from his pulsating nose. The concussion from my three old development ends, each with five unconstrained boxes of dynamite, had blown the ventilation doors out of my access tunnels all the way back to the shaft. He was clearly somewhat vexed. He stammered, "You weren't s'posed to blow the bloody doors off." Evidently, he had been watching too many films. I think the only reason he didn't fire me on the spot was that the mine was running short of qualified plonkers to inhabit the nether world, and he couldn't find a replacement anytime soon for my panel of ground. Suitably chastened, I sheepishly retreated back to my workplace and decided that it might be wise to dispose of the remaining old explosives with a little less enthusiasm.

I learned in the bar that a much-preferred approach, not mentioned in the rules but infinitely quicker, was to apply a water hose to the boxes and wash them into the drainage ditch that runs along every drive. It saved a lot of apprehension and explained why nobody else actually applied the five-stick approach from the handbook.

The company did not allow a single leave day to be taken in the first year of service. This is difficult to imagine today but seemed normal back then. After a year of continuous work, I jumped into Julia and hightailed it back to Jan Smuts airport, leaving her with key and ownership document on the driver's seat. I fondly imagined that the car thieves would be so surprised that a car would be left open and ready to go that, like a lady of easy virtue, she would rest there untouched for some months.

"I'm gonna miss you, you old dog," I murmured as I pecked her wing with an affectionate kiss and patted her bonnet. I span on my heel and walked reluctantly towards the sun setting over Terminal One.

Chapter 5: Camborne School of Mines

'Laboris Gloria Ludi' – Camborne School of Mines motto.

The English translation of the Camborne School of Mines motto is literally, 'The glory of work and play', but more accurately it's 'Work hard, play hard'. It was great to be back on English soil. The cold rain on my face made me feel energised and the taste of real IPA was fantastic. The only downside of IPA was that the English rugby team could drink more of it because it actually has a flavour, thereby enabling the South Africans and Aussies to beat us 'sauties' at the noble sport. You can't drink enough of their home grown horse piss to actually get hung over. The term 'sauty' was a term of endearment that the Afrikaner gave to the English-speaking South African, implying that he had one foot in the UK, the other in South Africa, and the end of his dick was getting salty in the sea.

I arrived in Cornwall to start further academic brainwashing. The lecturers at the school were a motley crew of characters who were probably unemployable in any other capacity. It was clear that they were a bunch of academics loosely held together by a central heating system. I fondly remember the welcoming speech from the deputy head of school; "You wash-ups are a complete bunch of tusses... It's a very good thing that the mining industry employs a lot of plonkers, because otherwise there'd be absolutely no hope for you wallies." Inspiring stuff. I knew I was in the right place and set about settling in.

I quickly found three other like-minded muckers and we rented a house in Camborne from Mrs. Orme. It was a dark and damp edifice and the basin in my room had a large, ominous-looking crack in it. The oil-fired AGA gave a tinge of warmth and a strong smell of oil, which combined comfortingly with the strong musty odour from the mushrooms growing on the wallpaper. In short, it was a wonderfully moist den of microbes which rapidly became our humble and much-loved bachelor pad. Relationships formed in such adversity generally stand the test of time and the muckers from those days are still great friends decades later. Clearly, there was something in the mushroom spores that bound people together for life. Perhaps they should start using them in marriage ceremonies.

Mrs. Orme wasn't quite the affable Cornish Piskie of first impression. At the end of the year, she deducted twenty quid from my deposit for the damage to the basin in my room. It was clear to me that this was a scam she applied to successive students, year on year, to extract a little extra pin money. I was not particularly impressed but decided to assist her in the replacement of the basin by isolating the water feeds and taking a four-pound hammer to it. I rapidly reduced it to tiny shards on the floor of my room and left her to the cleaning-up task. Twenty quid went a long way in those days.

Cornwall is one of the most beautiful places in England, and therefore the planet. The joys associated with sea, sand and continuous horizontal rain became a lifelong love affair for me. In Cornwall they say that you can predict the weather by standing at Land's End and gazing out towards the Isles of Scilly. If you can't see them, it's raining, and if you can ... it's about to rain.

As anywhere, it is, of course, important to learn the local dialect. Some may think that, as Cornwall is part of England, English would be the main language spoken, but that would be quite wrong. Rather like England and America, England and Cornwall are two places divided by a common language. To understand this, I will elucidate on some common words in Cornwallish so you won't be completely confused. Here are some essential words in all their glory:

Me 'Ansom

Everything and everyone can be 'ansom... or proper 'ansom if they are lucky. From an 'ansom meal to an 'ansom car, horse or pasty, 'ansom is a word that every Cornishman uses on a daily basis to describe something they like.

E

Some sentences start this way in Cornwallish. It can mean 'he/she' or 'you'. 'Awright ar e?' is a friendly greeting and means, 'Are you alright?' Often used in conjunction with 'me 'ansom' or 'me bird/lover/beauty/cheald (girl).'

'E' can also start a tale, as in; 'I'll tell e wot...' or alternatively, 'Wot 'appened wos...' This is the perfect phrase when you have some information to share or a point to emphasise.

Dreckly

Dreckly means that something will happen directly or later. However, the difference between dreckly and directly is that doing something 'dreckly' can take ages. There's no specified time limit, but it's likely to be much later than directly. What could be carried out today will probably be started next month. Indeed 'dreckly' is in effect 'mañana', but with less urgency. For example, in the context of finding out when someone is about to arrive at an appointment, deliver something, or complete an urgent task, it also translates as, 'When I am good and ready', with an undercurrent of, 'Don't worry, I'm on it' and a heavy hint of, 'Stop tapping your wrist, we don't do things that fast around here.'

Jumping

If you've made someone 'jumping' you'd better apologise, and not dreckly. This doesn't mean jumping for joy and is not an expression of happiness. If you meet someone looking disgruntled and they say they're jumping, especially if they're not obviously physically jumping, it means they're really angry. The good news is that this is most often heard in the past tense, as in, 'When she said that to me, I didn't know where to look, I was jumping!'

Proper Job

Only the Cornish can do a 'proper job' properly. Proper is most commonly paired with 'job' to form 'proper job'. A 'proper job' is anything that is done well. 'Proper job' is also an expression of appreciation, a confirmation of quality. Your new car is 'proper job' just as much as a tasty meal prepared by a loved one, especially a pasty, or any task that has been performed well. Very flexible with their slang, the Cornish.

I'm rufazrats

This means, 'I'm really hungover from all that Rattler I drank at the Plume' (or any local hostelry).

Wasson

A Cornishman's introduction, meaning, 'What's going on?' Who needs hello/hi/good morning/good evening when you can simply say, 'Wasson?' It's quicker and much more fun.

Radon (pronounced ride-on)

Radon means 'Right on.' A tricky one really, this is Cornish for 'yes/ideal/perfect' but also 'hello/goodbye/farewell' (try and get your head around that). This is a much more exciting and expressive affirmative than boring old 'Yes.' The highlighting and/or drawing out of vowels gives additional emphasis; 'Heading to the Countryman this weekend?' 'Radooon!'

Tuss

A word with its roots in old Cornish, it's thought to have some connection to male genitals but has become a general term of contempt. If called a tuss, either the person addressing you really doesn't like you, or they're so totally sure of your friendship that they're using it affectionately as a term of endearment or love.

Dearovim/Dearover

Contractions of 'dear of him' or 'dear of her', these terms crop up in the same way you might say, 'Bless their heart' at the end of a story in which someone has done something admirable or cute. Also used as a way of expressing sympathy for someone undergoing a rough time.

Teasy

Also spelt 'teazy', this is thought to derive from the Cornish word 'tesek', meaning hot-tempered or irritable, and that's exactly what it still means. Most commonly used to refer to a grumpy child, for example, 'Come on, you're only teasy 'cos you're tired.' When applied to an adult it effectively calls them out for being both tetchy and a big kid; if really teasy, you are teasy-assed, and if disliked you are a teasy-assed tuss.

Bleddy

Bleddy is an extremely Cornish way of pronouncing bloody, as in 'bloody hell.' It's more likely to be deployed as punctuation or a point of colourful emphasis in a sentence than in a wish to express anger. 'Bleddy' is synonymous with 'dammy' and can be combined with other Cornishisms: E's bleddy teasy.

Diddy?

Nothing to do with American rappers, this is a contraction of, 'Did he?' Diddy means either, 'Is that true?', 'Did you?' or 'Did he/she?' There's also, 'Diddah?' and 'Issuh?' which essentially mean the same thing.

Cousin Jack

Cousin Jack is a Cornishman who has left Cornwall to seek their fortune, often as a miner; it's also the name of a type of loading chute as mentioned earlier.

With the reader's newly acquired knowledge of Cornwallish the following should now make perfect sense:

"Wasson me 'ansum, awright ar e?"
Proper job, me beauty."
"Diddy see Cousin Jack at the Plume last night? E's rufazrats and proper teasy today. E's bleddy jumping cuz it's gone tits up in Oz, e should've dammy stayed at Crofty. Now

e's back at Mrs Orme's, dearover, got no bleddy sink, so e's a proper teasy-assed tuss. Radooooon my lover, see e dreckly..."

So, to the serious business of education; the Mining Engineering course at Camborne School of Mines demanded a good deal of effort. I listened jealously to my mates from high school who complained about the four, three or even two hours of lectures that they attended each week on their 'History of Sponge Bob' or 'Tourist beaches of the Arctic' courses. At Camborne, we attended a forty-hour lecture week and often had to write up experiment and test results during evenings and over weekends. This wasn't the walk in the park I had fondly imagined when I signed up to MEAT – it had turned out to be uphill both ways. Of course, a major benefit of the curriculum was that I was being paid to do it. This income, along with the meagre savings from my gold-mining year, funded an intense lifestyle of beers, books and bonking. On reflection, I wouldn't have had it any other way.

One regular Friday afternoon activity for a number of the fifty odds and sods in the class who had to attend double surveying was, on completion of the attendance register, to quietly slip out of the back of the room, one by one, and leg it to the Plume of Feathers public house a hundred yards away for a prolonged afternoon session. I often wonder if the lecturer, Ron Hooper, knew we did this.

Hooper was a wry Cornishman who was as sharp as a whip. I remember him catching me out once on the survey course. He noted that my theodolite reading errors were the same as those of mining lecturer and World War II fighter pilot John Shrimpton, who had graciously given me a helping hand. Hooper didn't fail me for this, but the guy who light tabled his copy of the chain survey upside down, thereby inverting the whole of King Edward Mine didn't quite make the grade and was failed. Shrimpton, a decorated war hero, didn't take the teaching process too seriously. I once saw him whiting out the date on his notes (the date was sometime in the 1940s) just before photocopying them to give out in one of his lectures. Mining methodologies, machinery and technology had moved on somewhat since then. To give you a sense of the ancient experiential base we were learning from, I quote from Ron Hooper's book on surveying, a book we were all required to read, where he states, quite seriously, that the "use of a candle for lighting underground should not be sniffed at." Presumably in case you got too close and sniffed it out, and, amid the waft of burning hair, ended up completely in the dark... a state that I regularly found myself in during his lectures.

Chapter 6: More Gold in South Africa

'Stars only shine in the dark.' – D H Sidebottom

Between my first and second year at the Camborne School of Mines, I returned to work at the Kloof gold mine, driven by the very real need to replenish my bank account. The first year had been taxing in the extreme and, having become used to a reasonably large disposable income as a miner, I'd neglected to notice as a student that consuming industrial quantities of ale was a bank account depleting pastime. I had a choice – work or starve.

On arrival in Johannesburg, I was whisked off by Van to renew my old acquaintance with the Jolly Rogerer, the drinking den in the Hillbrow district. In South Africa at the time, homosexuality was banned. I was reliably informed that there had been no 'queen in the country' since independence. Despite this there were just as many of those who prefer to bat with their own sex as in any other place on the planet, and good luck to them. To my mind, they decreased competition for the fairer sex by reducing the number of interested parties. I also noted without rancour that they generally dressed far more stylishly and were a lot better-looking than me.

The Jolly Rogerer had become something of a haven for these guys, not that I had realised it at first. Still being young and naïve, I thought that the bloke in a frilly pink tutu was surely on his way to a stag party. He approached us. His sashay was impressive. He really was taking this drag thing very seriously. He did a phenomenal catwalk impression, swinging his pink umbrella with some panache. I looked around to see if we hadn't somehow stumbled into a fashion shoot. No, but the place had noticeably quietened, and Van had fixed the approaching tutu with an implacable stare from his remaining eye. I suddenly got the sense that all was not quite as it seemed. Something was about to happen.

Mr. Tutu wafted up and extended one hand to Van's v-neck shirt, where his chest hair sprung exuberantly from the notch. That hand pinched a bunch of this hair and twisted it nonchalantly.

"Ooooo, that's nice," said the tutu.

I can only begin to imagine what was going through Van's addled brain as he tried to register this assault on his person. It's difficult to read a one-eyed man's face, but this was clearly an experience completely outside of his strict Christian Afrikaner upbringing. What I think I saw was an expression of total disbelief pass across his countenance, followed by dismay, irritation and anger, all in less than a second. I expected a brawl. There was a short silence. I think I heard a fly stomping across the bar, or maybe it was the blood thumping through my temples.

"Fuck off, you shirt-lifting fudge-packing fairy," said Van. Mr Tutu's face turned crimson and the veins in his neck visibly pulsated. A tic twitched on one side of his mouth. The silence deepened.

The tutu-clad man tossed his head back with a flamboyant air and brought up his pink umbrella. Here we go, I thought, mentally preparing myself for the ensuing brawl, for there was no Gentle Pete to protect me today. He softly brought the rolled umbrella down on Van's shoulder in the manner of the Queen of England creating a knight of the realm, or a fairy waving a magic wand.

"Turn to shit," he intoned. "Turn to shit." And he swiftly twirled and minced away.

The onlookers broke into a chorus of laughter and applause, and the tension instantly eased. Honours even, we proceeded to drink the evening away as if nothing had happened, although I feel Van may have been somewhat shaken by the idea that he was the object of such attention.

Once a short re-induction at the mine had reacquainted me with safety procedures, how to blow stuff up, and, for some bizarre reason, snake recognition, I was sent back underground to wrest gold from the bowels of the earth. It felt strangely like home. It was great to be away from the shackles of schooling in the art of mining, where the danger of dying from terminal boredom was high. Far better to be down in the trenches where real metal was won, real lives risked, and real bullshit created. On the coalface, as it were. South African mining was high risk in those days, but in our twenties, we thought we were invincible. However, the accidents I saw in those formative years gave me huge pause for thought, and I like to think that as my career advanced, I applied safer ways of going about the business.

The dangers involved in the South African mines in the early 1980s should not be underestimated. During my first year, Kloof had fifty-two fatalities and countless maiming injuries. Some were due to explosive releases of pressure, some to falls of ground, but most were due to human stupidity and error. It gave me a lifelong belief in the need for toolbox safety briefings for every shift, along with risk assessments for every task, a discipline to stop and fix any problem, and the absolute need for vigilance by every single person. I truly believe that every accident is preventable with the right engineering design approach and the right attitude.

Whilst I was trying to lessen the risk to my team, I noted that others were applying different approaches. I descended back into the bowels of the earth with a contract to blast development headings in front of the stopes of a miner called Thinus van Schalkwyk. Thinus was a modestly efficient miner who lived extremely well. He seemed to have more possessions than befitting a man of his station and productivity. He managed to run expensive cars and mistresses and he also had a penchant for expensive sunglasses. The latter made him look like a bit of a dick going underground, but each to his own.

I was quickly made aware of how he had achieved this. Once underground at his crib station, he would don a doctor's white coat, drape a stethoscope around his neck, and replace his hardhat with a surgical cap. He had built a secluded office behind wooden panels. Once ensconced, he turned around a sign on a string, stating, 'The doctor will see you now.' Inside, he cut up coloured chalks into large pills and sold them to his crew as a cure-all for anything from the common cold to erectile dysfunction... a service for which his crew paid considerable sums from their bonuses and for which (unusually for miners) they brought cash underground.

The scams of the South African miner in those days knew no bounds.

Chapter 7: The Camborne School of Mines Club

"The rules are simple – there are none." – Shonda Rhimes

The Camborne School of Mines Club was the centre of our social sphere at the school. It was interesting to observe that many of the city and suburban folk on the mining course had complained that there was nothing to do in Cornwall when they first arrived. By the end of the three years, there wasn't a single person who wanted to leave. They had found their niche, their centre of interest; they made their own entertainment and had, in their own way, become self-sufficient. This was another of the many benefits of the School of Mines, albeit one that was more by accident than design.

The club in my day was a place of considerable alcohol consumption. To initiate new recruits there was an induction night called Smokers' Night. The recollection of my own induction is somewhat vague due to copious quantities of brain-fuzz juice. I can only surmise that the mind likes to blank out such fun and games. Suffice it to say, there were a series of increasingly outrageous drinking games that made beer pong look like the Sunday school picnic that it is. The one that still sticks in my mind was the Dance of the Flaming Arseholes. In this game, a metre length of toilet paper was stuffed into the competitor's bum crack and set alight. He needed to then drink his pint before removing the burning paper, a searing incentive to drink it down fast. It was a baptism of fire on many levels. I am reliably informed that this is now banned and never, ever takes place...

Another form of entertainment was the tradition of a naked conga that formed towards the end of the evening. The conga wended its way from the club, through the chill waters of Camborne fountain (shrinking the mini Jack somewhat more) and through Tyacks Hotel in the centre of town, where custom dictated that the local ladies would gather to check out the talent before the conga repaired back to the club. The local constabulary turned a blind eye to this public show of indecency. I believe that many a relationship commenced shortly after this blatant advertising ploy. In my year, there was a small article in a national newspaper about this strange 'pagan' ritual. To my regret, I do not have a cutting, but it gave us some degree of misplaced pride, whilst vexing the Principal of the school. No wonder he was hell-bent on getting the school tied to Exeter University as quickly as he could, thereby creating a degree of deniability for himself, while losing the independence of this wonderful ancient mining institution.

It was once said that there was a Cornishman at the bottom of every hole in the world, and I believe there was some truth in that. The Camborne School of Mines students believed with some justification that they were the real miners, who happily did proper engineering, got their hands dirty and solved real-world problems. Such an august body of men and women needed to have a rival. Fortunately, there is another, equally old, 'mining' school in London, where they teach speed knitting, unicorn worship, and fantasy wedding dress design. Or so I assume. Quite why the royal family should think it a good idea to sponsor a mining school where there are no mines is quite the imponderable. Then again, maybe it's not that surprising looking at the current crop of royals. Still, the rival school does provide some good sport, and practice for our rugby team when they hand the Royals their annual thrashing.

Several of our lecturers took part in the activities of the CSM Club. John Hignett was one such participant, who had retired from active mining life to run a small farm in Cornwall, whilst supplementing his meagre farming income by torturing students with complex engineering problems. Before his time with CSM, John had developed the Channel Tunnel between England and France. He was a font of useful wisdom on tunnelling, particularly when plied with a pint or two.

The most fascinating story I recall from John's lectures was his tale about the holing through of the Channel Tunnel. In the project, the French bored two tunnels towards England and the British developed two tunnels towards France. When the tunnels were within four hundred metres of each other, the British had to drill a pilot hole into the French tunnel to ensure that everything lined up. As a matter of interest and record, the error in alignment was less than twenty centimetres, a phenomenal feat of surveying prowess in a tunnel thirty kilometres long. I can only imagine that Ron Hooper's candles and canaries were on top form in those days, and he did a proper job. But back to John; his job was to drill the pilot hole, which to the immense chagrin of his French counterparts, he called the garlic sniffer.

Now, John Hignett sometimes indulged in one or two pints. One night at the Club, he had consumed one or two more than was strictly advisable. We had heard that the rozzers were out in force breathalysing the merry folk of Camborne, so we confiscated John's car keys and poured him into a taxi. The night, however, was still young and one of our number remarked that John's car, a Mini Cooper, might fit between the columns of the entrance to the Club. Sure enough, a survey tape confirmed that the car was 373 cm (12' 3") and the distance between the columns was 378 cm (12' 5"). A near-perfect fit. It's interesting to note that eight mining students, fuelled by forty beers, can not only outdrink the medics from the Royal School of Mines, but they are also capable of lifting a Mini Cooper and placing it gently, if somewhat snugly, between the stone columns of the CSM Club. In the morning, John was jumping which obviously added to the fun. We did with a little ingenuity manage to recover his car for him. It was a lot harder without our evening fuel.

John got his own back, of course. The very next Saturday morning we woke to find that an enormous pile of cow shit had been dumped in the same entrance of the Club,

with a small sign on top of it: "Never Bullshit a Bullshitter."
Lessons from the school came 24/7.

Chapter 8: Diamonds in South Africa

"A lump of coal is just a lump of carbon; a diamond is a lump of carbon that has been subject to heat, stress and pressure. Elementally, they are the same." – Jack Shaft

On summer vacations most of the Camborne School of Mines crew were filling large bags with sand from a sandpit somewhere in southern England, close to a pub, for what is euphemistically called 'work experience'. I, on the other hand, hopped on a plane back to South Africa to make use of my hard-won blasting ticket and make some headway against the drinking debt that had built up over the previous nine months of desk-bound servitude. University was to me, for the most part, a privileged glimpse of the bleeding obvious or learning something so esoteric that it would never be of any possible use to anyone apart from an academic, who would teach it to another generation of pathologically bored soon-to-be engineers. I couldn't wait to get back to the real world of blood, sweat and beers.

For my second vacation, I was lucky enough to find myself at the Premier Diamond Mine at Cullinan, the place where the largest gem diamond in the world had been found. The Cullinan Diamond is without a doubt the most famous diamond and by far the largest clear rough diamond ever discovered. As a matter of interest, the rough stone had four smooth sides, indicating that it had been part of an even larger stone originally. Most diamonds were formed over 3 billion years ago deep within the Earth's crust under conditions of intense heat and pressure that cause carbon atoms to crystallise.

The Cullinan Diamond was found five metres below the surface by Frederick Wells, surface manager at the mine, on 26 January 1905. It was approximately 10 cm long, 6.3 cm wide and 6 cm deep, and weighed 3,106 carats (621.2 grams which is the weight of half a pint of IPA in an imperial 1 pint glass including the weight of the glass). The cut stones from this behemoth are found in the Crown Jewels today. A slightly larger black stone, the Sergio had been found in Brazil on the surface in 1895 and like all other black diamonds is believed to be of meteoric origin. The Sergio with its' distinctive lack of clarity was therefore far less valuable but muscled in 60 carats heavier (that's12 grams, or three teaspoons of sugar) for a total of 3,167 carats (half a pint of Guinness in a pint glass). It was broken into small fragments and used as industrial diamond drill bits. The third largest stone found so far, the Sewelo, weighs in at a 'mere' 1758 carats (a half full half pint glass) and was found at the Karowe mine, Botswana, in 2019. Clearly all these half full glasses, whilst weighing the right amount, are twice the size they need to be.

By the time I arrived in Cullinan, the mine was deep underground and the production areas were large open stopes mined with long blast holes and mucked from draw points at the base of the stopes. My main task was to break the large rocks that occasionally blocked off the draw points. These oversized rocks prevented the ore flowing to the rail mounted loaders which would fling the muck into wagons behind them. Some of these intransigent rocks were the size of small houses and the method for breaking them was to jam 25 kg bags of ANFO (Ammonium Nitrate and Fuel Oil) against each mammoth rock. ANFO is a secondary explosive material which we ignited using dynamite boosters and electric detonators. On my first shift, one of my draw points jammed up with a monster. My gang of workers set about with great zeal spragging large numbers of 25kg bags against the offending rock with boosters.

I guess I should have realised that something was up from the massive cheesy grins of my crew, but I put it down to enthusiasm for my English, more democratic style of leadership, and my Umbala speeches. Blasting of the rocks blocking a draw point happened at the end of the shift. By the end of my first shift, my crew had charged the larger rocks with a store-depleting quantity of powder. I connected the electric detonators by a long cable into a blasting point two hundred metres down the drive and, importantly, around a corner. As the authorised miner, it was my duty to initiate the blast when I was satisfied that every person was clear of the blasting area. I undertook a thorough inspection, checking each and every drive and cubby to ensure no dozing miner was left behind. My crew watched with mounting expectation as we stood near the blasting point, waiting for the whistles to signal that all areas were clear. The whistles shrilled, and my hand moved toward the blasting button. My hand slowed slightly, and I hesitantly looked towards the crew... They were all hunched over close to the ground with their fingers pushed very firmly into their ears and their eyes screwed tightly shut, clearly braced for the forthcoming concussion. Unfortunately, I already had some momentum towards the button, and as I hit it, I squeezed my eyes shut and hunched my shoulders. A massive air blast hit us. It lifted me off my feet and threw me along the drive in a well-performed swallow dive. I hit the ground with a crunching thud, reminiscent of the sickening thumps I had become accustomed to feeling when playing rugby at the gold mines. I lost my dignity and helmet, and gained a rather unsightly facial 'road rash'.

The crew were also lying around on the drive. They were there not because of the concussion, but because they were laughing so hard that they couldn't contain their mirth. Ten grown men were rolling around in the mud like pigs at an orgy, crying with laughter. This laughter was to follow me all the way back to the shaft and change house. In the bar that evening, I learned that there is a recommended technique for hitting the blasting button. This involves shoving your thumbs into your ears, performing an elk impression, and using a forefinger to press it whilst hunching low and bracing against the concussion. The crew got to love my 'moo' just before a blast and I am happy to say that the rest of the summer flew by without major incident.

Chapter 9: The Piggy and the Presidency

"I am fond of pigs. Dogs look up at you, cats look down on you, but pigs look you straight in the eye." – Winston Churchill

Probably the most renowned incident during my time at Camborne School of Mines was the one involving the pig. The story has resonated down the annals of time to the extent that people still talk about it in awe, even today. The event happened in my final year when, as a joke, I decided to stand for election as President of the Students' Union. A little like the Monster Raving Loony Party in the UK, I thought to act as a spoiler candidate to prevent the more serious contender, Raymond, from assuming the position unopposed and the consequent power of popularity going to his head.

Of course, to take part in any such critical election it was important to make a manifesto, one that would appeal to the student population. The muckers drinking with me in the Club on the evening we decided to put my name forward came up with an A-Z of policies. Here are some of my personal favourites from the A-Z manifesto of the DUMB (Drink U More Beer) Student Union Presidential candidate (me).

C. CAPITAL punishment is an anathema. It is unfair to people from London.

D. DAILY DRINKING of beer will be obligatory for CSM students in order to build tolerance for your forthcoming need to run projects on a heady mix of alcohol, caffeine and adrenaline.

F. FRIVOLITY is one of our values and a Serious Frivolity Office will be established in the Students' Union.

G. GILBERT and Sullivan Society productions will improve. There will be real cannons in their on-location production of The Pirates of Penzance to make it more authentic.

H. HALVES are for visiting Royal School of Mines students. Real engineers drink pints.

O. OPPORTUNITIES will be the new name for problems. We don't have drinking problems; we have drinking opportunities.

Q. QUITTERS from the Camborne School of Mines should not start in the first place in order to improve their self-esteem. Clearly, this is one of the functions of Smokers' Night.

R. ROUNDS. Every man (and woman) will stand his or her round in fair turn.

S. SHOTS are mandatory beer chasers on special occasions, such as still being alive after the night before.

V. VOMITORIUM. This splendid invention of the Romans will be re-introduced at the CSM Club.

W. WORK is the curse of the drinking classes. No educational activities will take place after lectures.

Z. ZEBRA crossings will be made available to all animals wishing to cross the road, especially the large number of CSM students on their way to the Plume of Feathers on a Friday afternoon.

Raymond was a bit of an arrogant prick. He'd read how the Roman consul wouldn't campaign for election on the grounds that the perfect leader was one who didn't seek power; however, he had neglected to read the small print where he would have noted the need for underlings to campaign on the candidate's behalf. Or maybe he was just lazy and thought he was a shoo-in given the paucity of the competition.

Very shortly after publishing my manifesto, things started going wrong. Unknown to me, another student came into the running against Raymond. He was a serious contender with policies such as more frequent buses to Truro and expanding the sports agenda. I don't think it was all about politics for him either since he really didn't get along with Raymond. I could see myself supporting him.

Unfortunately, it was too late to drop out, so I became the neutral candidate as the supporters of my two opponents polarised the student body. I had gone in with the attitude that it wasn't really an important position and the only people who cared about it were doing it only for their CVs. Since I wanted to be a miner and already had some mining experience, I doubted being Student President would have any meaning for me. I set up my campaign HQ in the Club and borrowed another campaign strategy from the Romans: buy your potential voters beer.

Suffice it to say that, with such a populist agenda and campaign strategy, the other candidates didn't stand a chance, and I acceded to the Office of President on the back of a landslide, if you'll forgive the geological term. This predominantly figurehead position allowed my buddies and me to orchestrate almost nightly parties and events, steering me in the direction of my ultimate dream - to build an English pub in France and retire, using the time to write a set of unreliable stories and anecdotes masquerading as an   autobiography.

I am happy today that there was no social media during my youth; it would probably have ensured I would be as unemployable back then as I am likely to be on the publication of this book. If you are reading this, I have probably retired to the Frog and Bulldog, a sound British drinking establishment nestling in the Pyrenees mountains to which you are all invited. First pint free, vote for me!

Despite my father's desire of a proper profession for me, I managed to stumble into the nearest thing to it, for drinking has been part of English mining culture going back to before the Dark Ages. In medieval times, when establishing a new village, they first found a mineral outcrop, then a built a pub to house, feed and refresh the workers. Having completed the pub, they would then build a church right next door. Since those days, there is genuine justification for the claim that the pub has always been the social centre for British life, as an institution that comes even before the church. Indeed, a little-known fact is that the Queen of England is not only the Head of Church and State, but also Landlady-in-Chief.

A book called The Pub and the People published during the late 1930s identifies the quintessential pub ethos where working men gathered in the vault. The vault was a shiny, long bar counter haloed on the floor with a six-inch wide strip of sawdust, where customers would spit, spill beer and throw up. Hence, the term 'spit and sawdust' to describe a good, basic, working-class public house. The author lists the activities that took place there and elsewhere in the pub: talking, thinking, smoking, spitting, playing games, betting, singing, playing the piano, buying and selling goods including hot pies and bootlaces... and, of course, drinking. Not much had changed in the intervening years at the Camborne School of Mines Club.

The pub is a sanctuary where an English person can get away from the crackpot, mumbo-jumbo and politically-correct dodgy information fed to us by the mainstream media's so-called experts, scientists, nodding donkeys, politicians, journalists and jumped-up students of polygraphy and fashion science. It is worth noting that a student of polygraphy would have a field day with the audio version of this book, assuming of course, that I was the voice.

In a proper English pub, you can find out everything that's wrong with the world for the cost of a pint of ale. Just start a conversation with the middle-aged man in the baggy jumper, who is wearing either sensible shoes, or socks and sandals. He's probably called Ronald. Avoid Borises and Jacobs, they might be batshit crazy. As long as his glass doesn't dry out, Ronald will happily tell you all his ideas about how to set the world straight, which might include the following:

Get rid of participation trophies; it is political correctness gone mad! We're not getting them ready for the real world so, no, Timmy, you can't get a gold star for running in the egg-and-spoon race. It cheapens Oliver's medal for winning; try harder next time, you little shit.

Bring back caning. The problem with schools is there isn't any discipline - my teachers used to cane me, and I (twitch, twitch) turned out alright.

Kids these days are too reliant on technology. They whine on and on about global warming from their air-conditioned classrooms. They protest about fossil-fuel use from their multimedia-enhanced schools, which they got to in their family's gas-guzzling SUVs on traffic-choked roads. They complain that they are bored whilst staring mindlessly at YouTube videos on the TVs found in every room of their house beaming idiotic reality shows of other peoples' moronic lives. Turn off the TV, get off yer iPhone and onto yer bike. Come down the pub where you can meet real people and start actually living.

We need to go back to basics: the three Rs: Reading, wRiting and aRithmetic, not this meaningless 'coding' nonsense, or 'new maths'. In the new approach, it's more important to know what you are doing rather than actually get the right answer. Bugger being in the right ballpark, as long as the workings show the right process. And we wonder why they are unemployable.

Kids these days don't know what a stiff upper lip is, well I'll tell you, it's what got us through the war. Jerry was trying to bomb us into submission, but the plucky Brit kept his back straight, his chin up, and carried on! These days they'd want to talk about how the constant risk of death, claustrophobic shelters and sudden explosions made them feel! Send 'em to the mines, I say.

Bring back capital punishment; it's the only language these reprobates understand, yeah, we might get it wrong occasionally, but it does have a very low recidivism rate.

Conversation starters guaranteed to excite some interest from the woolly-jumpered mammoths include topics such as:

Don't you think... men should all talk about our feelings and that would make things better, or, speed cameras make our country safer, or, water should be sold in bottles or, salad is a meal, or, everyone has asthma, allergies and ADHD.

So, the Frog and Bulldog Pub in the mind's eye of my retirement is a place for group therapy and setting the world right. As an aside, saying "Pub?" to me is the human equivalent of saying "Walkies?" to a dog: I get all excited, wag my tail and start running in circles. Now, where is my baggiest jumper…?

On to the pig. For reasons long forgotten, a group of drunken cohorts in the club, led by a character that (to avoid any potential legal proceedings) I will fondly describe as 'Pat the Planet Pillager', decided to commandeer a pig from a local farmyard. Quite how they got this full-grown sow into the back of a car, transported it along Camborne High Street in the dead of night (past the other sleeping porkies), broke into the school and re-penned it in the principal's office without setting off any alarms remains highly classified. Today, there would have been CCTV footage to review and no doubt social-media bragging that would also inevitably uncover the culprits.

Peter Hackett, the principal and victim of this prank, was livid. He called me into his office and tried every which way to make me divulge the identity of the perpetrators. He tried to bribe me, cajole me and even threatened to expel me for being an accessory. Whilst many in the student body knew who the perpetrators were, I am proud to say that we stood as one in protective silence, and nobody faced the threatened consequences. The pig became emblematic of the school. I recall seeing pig stickers all over the London Underground for several years after, and even one on the nose of an aircraft at Luton Airport. Much later in life, I made a short documentary about the school and interviewed Peter Hackett about the incident. He was more sanguine by that time, but still desperately wanted to know who had done it; although he had a few clues by then, as far as I know, he hasn't yet found out.

Era 2

The Real Mining Years – from Miner to Underground Manager

"If you have a nut allergy, the mining industry is not for you."
– Jack Shaft

Chapter 10: The Cornish Tin Mines

"The light at the end of the tunnel is not always the shift boss – it could be a train coming." – Jack Shaft

My first real job after my time at the Camborne School of Mines was a trundle down the road, in Cornwall. I had developed an unlikely friendship with the CEO of the local tin mines, Brian Calver. Brian was a salt-of-the-earth cockney, with a penchant for pails full of lager. I guess that's how you could tell he was from the Royal School of Mines - a real miner would be drinking real ale. Brian offered me a job at the Wheal Jane mine, to start immediately after the summer holidays following graduation.

The senior management, all of them from the Royal School of Mines, decided to throw the new blood from Camborne in at the deep end. About 1000m straight down in fact. My first three months were spent in the loading pocket. This is the transfer point at the bottom of a vertical shaft where rocks are loaded by bin, hopper and chute into a skip for lifting to the surface. I learned to press three buttons in sequence to fill the skips with ore as they came in line with the chutes. I can only assume that Royal School of Mines graduates find this work stimulating, but the rigours of Camborne tended to weed out such people. Even a Luddite with such limited computing capacity as I possessed could do this without complication and I quickly sussed out that the cycle time between loads was ninety seconds. This knowledge enabled me to do the job without looking up whilst reading a book. Don't tell me men can't multitask.

Just as I was in danger of resigning on account of life-threatening tedium and a lack of books, the powers that be let me loose with the Cornish miners, and I was put on shovelling and tramming duties. Tramming involved moving rocks using an electric loco to pull a train of wagons filled with broken ore from Cousin Jack loading chutes under the operating orebodies back to ore passes at the shaft. The wagons were tipped into the passes to fill the chutes that loaded the skips. A Cousin Jack is also the name for a Cornish miner you will recall. Clearly the Royal School of Mines brass thought I should learn the process from skip to orebody in small steps. Perhaps they had read my school reports.

I was put with a trammer called Paddy O'Toole. Paddy was the stereotypical embodiment of an Irishman. Some days I could have sworn he was playing a deliberate caricature. He was as happy as a dog with two dicks if he had a plate of potatoes, a pint of Guinness, and an audience for his many yarns.

One day Paddy and I were tramming some ore from a stope with rocks the size of small cars. The stope miner had drilled the blast holes too far apart in order to save time. As a result, we had problems getting them through the chutes and into the wagons, and so we had to blast the rocks in the chute to break them into smaller sizes. It was tedious work, but the real problems arose at the shaft ore pass tip, where a grizzly prevented large rocks entering the pass. A grizzly is a large mesh made with steel rails welded together, creating a massive sieve with roughly fifty-centimetre-square holes through which the rocks would pass. The grizzly prevents large rocks jamming the pass. On this day, we were having all sorts of problems getting the oversized rocks through it.

Paddy was regularly climbing out onto the grizzly and clearing the rocks with a pinch bar (a large wrecking bar) or a 14 lb (6 kg) hammer, while I was running backwards and forwards to the stope to continue collecting another load. We thought we were doing well, but the shift boss, nicknamed "Woofer" (he started every sentence with a growl and ended it with a woof) was not impressed with our productivity. The first time I had met Woofer, when I was assigned to his shift as a trammer, he greeted me in standard production-oriented fashion:

"Grrrr... look 'ere boy," he said, "if you tram they tonnes set in the mine call (the production target for the month), I'll fill yer pockets so full of cash, you'll have to turn sideways to get out the mine gate. Woof." Quite an offer for a young graduate. "Umbala," I murmured to myself.

However, back to the grizzly. Woofer arrived on his regular inspection of the workplace just as Paddy was taking a big swing with the hammer at a particularly intransigent rock. He went apoplectic. All we heard for the first minute was a series of explosive growls and barks that brought to mind a demented Doberman. Eventually he calmed down enough to growl, "Grrr... Paddy, tie up to the safety lanyard block... Grrr... don't end up down the pass... woof woof." Paddy climbed off the grizzly. He hadn't been harnessed to the fall arrest system (a safety device that resembles a large-scale car seatbelt), and had thus running the risk of falling into the ore pass. Incidentally, this would be an unlikely occurrence due to the large quantity of potatoes and Guinness in Paddy's past which had made him somewhat circumferentially endowed.

I had already cottoned on to the fact that it is a good idea to make oneself scarce when steam was coming out of a shift bosses ears; I quickly jumped into the loco and drove the wagons out to the stopes for yet another load. Woofer continued his stream of barks as I lumbered gratefully out of sight and hearing. I knew that Woofer would be passing me shortly, and so I set about filling the wagons with energetic enthusiasm. Woofer, when he did pass, went by with nary a sideways glance, though growls, barks and steam were still emanating from him, bringing to mind the last voyage of Turner's The Fighting Temeraire. Unlike the Temeraire however, I knew he would be returning shortly, after inspecting the stopes.

Woofer passed me on his way back, just as I was filling the last wagon. I was happy to note he seemed a little less vexed, woofing a cheery goodbye. I finished loading the wagons and, moving a bit faster given my electric locomotion, we arrived back at the ore pass together. If

Paddy's previous conduct had turned Woofer into a steamship, the behaviour we now witnessed made him blow a boiler. Woofer surpassed all previous explosions. Paddy had clearly misunderstood the instruction to tie up to the safety lanyard fall arrest system and was standing in the middle of the grizzly, applying himself to the offending rocks. The tightly tied handle of the hammer was secured to the safety block.

"Well, at least we would save the tools, if not the O'Toole." I remarked. Woofer was not amused.

Six months of tramming, shovelling, and breaking rocks passed by. It did cross my mind, once or twice, that prisoners probably spent less time chained up and breaking rocks than we did. At least we were paid for the privilege and, although never having to turn sideways to get out of the mine gate, I did get to sink a few ales in the local pubs and talk fondly about Woofer. He was a renowned local character; despite his gruff exterior, he actually had a heart of gold and cared greatly for the safety of his people.

My next stop on the Royal School of Mines training programme, clearly designed to break graduates from the superior school, was at a development end as a driller and blaster. I was put under the wing of Reggie Tellum, a silver-haired Cornishman who had been mining long before I was a twinkle in my father's eyes. Reggie, who referred to me as his "Bleddy student", was a highly talented driller, who could run two rock drills at the same time, balancing them perfectly with the respective air legs (an air-operated support for a rock drill). The drill steel would stay perfectly at centre in the drill hole and so we rarely had stuck drill rods, a common problem in the Wheal Jane ground conditions. Reggie was fifty-six the day I joined the mines, and fifty-six the day I left, three years later. The reality was that he was well beyond retirement age, but everyone maintained the illusion that he wasn't so that he could continue doing what he loved. I learned a vast amount from Reggie, and I still maintain to this day that there isn't much I don't know about development end mining thanks to his fatherly guidance.

Reggie did have one bad habit however, which was to put fishplate bends in the tracks, rather than bending the rails to go around corners. The fishplate is the plate of steel that ties together the rails on which the locomotive runs. Of course, as his offsider, at the time I connived with this heinous mining practice. However, nine months later, he was extremely irritated when, as the relief shift boss, I forced him to replace the fishplates and bend the track properly. I was always a "bleddy student" to him and I am sure that, even in my middle years, he would still greet me as such.

After Reggie's education, I spent a few months stoping. Over a few short weeks, the physical burden of dragging a rock drill and air leg up into the stopes slowly transformed from what seemed a Herculean task to a matter of fact, five-minute, start-of-shift chore. This was the time in my life when I had never been fitter or physically stronger. It's been a rapid downhill slide ever since. It was about eighteen months into my trial by brutality, in what the management probably thought of as a superlative graduate training programme, that I earned my first stripe on the management ladder and became a relief shift boss. Shift bosses are the corporals of the mining army, promoted due to whip-sharp cunning, Umbala-style inspiring leadership and an ability to read without moving their lips. The collective pronoun for a gathering of shift bosses is a gaggle (okay, I made that up, but it fits well). The cacophony and hustle and bustle in the shift boss' office at shift change is similar to geese at feeding time, or Mumbai's central train station at rush hour; it's a noisy, smelly melee of confused organisation. I loved every minute of it.

Graduating through the ranks to shift boss had all sorts of ramifications. It's always difficult to become the boss of someone whom you have worked alongside for some time. As the relief shift boss, I was the guy who filled in for those who were on leave. Despite the claim by many that nightshifts are OK and you get used to them, the truth is that nightshifts are never pleasant. The permanent shift bosses would invariably arrange to take as much of their leave as possible over the nightshift part of their scheduled cycle. I therefore spent a lot of time as a young shift boss working relief nightshifts. Of course, when you're underground it doesn't matter when the sun rises, since mines work twenty-four-seven.

One rule that applies to every mine in which I have ever worked is that it is forbidden to sleep underground. This wasn't a problem on day or afternoon shifts, but became problematic on nightshifts, and particularly when changing over from days or afternoons. In the early days of my shift bossdom, I witnessed quite a few miners at the resting place (crib station) who, at my approach would flutter their eyelids and mutter "Amen" to convey the myth that they had been lost in prayer. The challenge for the novice shift boss promoted from the ranks was how to gain respect from those guys without firing someone and making yourself deeply unpopular.

Oddly enough, my chance to solve this problem arose when I was filling in for Woofer, who had taken leave so he could bark at people on the Spanish Riviera. I can't even begin to imagine how that went. We couldn't understand much of what he usually said, and we shared a common tongue.

One time, on the second day of the nightshift cycle, I visited the tramming level. I happily noted that the now well-harnessed Paddy was breaking rock with gay abandon. I started off down the drive towards the stopes. About two hundred yards down I caught a glimpse of a man sleeping inside a large metal ventilation column stored on the floor of a crosscut (access passageway). Shit. If I woke him up, I would have no choice but to fire him. If I didn't fire him, everybody would see me as a soft touch, and lose respect.

This had the smell of an intractable problem, but I certainly couldn't let sleeping miners lie.

I decided to wander back to the ore pass. Maybe the guy would wake up and disappear. As I was perambulating, it struck me that Paddy was my answer.

"Paddy, come here a minute, will you? Take off that harness, but keep your hammer and come with me..." We got within fifty yards of the offending miner. "Right," I said to him in a hushed tone, "I want you to go along to the next crosscut, as quietly as a mouse on tiptoes, and then flatten the large vent column lying there as quickly as you can with your hammer. I will be waiting here for you to keep out of the way." He clearly thought I had gone insane.

He walked along the drive, muttering to himself about how shift bossing power had clearly gone to my head and asking why he was having to endure pointless tasks. Two minutes later, the first loud bang rang out. The sleeping miner clearly thought his end had come. He shot out of the end of the vent duct like a scalded jackrabbit. He was travelling faster than a Ferrari as he passed me, now standing with my lamp turned off to the side of the main drive. He got to the shaft in Olympic time and then started to catch his breath. Paddy was laughing ready to burst. I strolled up to him and picked his sobbing form off the ground; tears had cut a trail through the dust of his cheeks, creating clean rivulets on his grimy face. He tried to say something to me. I stopped him. I didn't want to know. It was better if I just let the story find its own way around. I never had another man sleep on my shift for the rest of my time at Wheal Jane.

Chapter 11: GBH

"If someone is accused of Grievous Bodily Harm, they are accused of causing very serious physical injury to someone."
– Collins English Dictionary

After a few months of substituting on the nightshift, I became a regular shift boss with my own full-time crew. Shift bossing has been one of my favourite jobs. It's all real-time problem-solving, and at the end of the shift, you hand over to someone else who takes up the cudgel to beat up whatever problems and challenges you have left them. You forget about the challenges until you come in the next day to face a whole raft of new ones, and so the cycle goes on. There isn't really any long-term challenge to it though, and you sleep soundly knowing that by the next day the problems are inevitably long gone.

I had one particular miner on my crew whose nickname amongst middle management was GBH. Rumour had it that he had spent considerable jail time for grievous bodily harm. Judging by the look of the bloke, my distinct impression was that there must be more than a grain of truth to the story. To give a bit more colour to the character, GBH was one of the few Cornishmen I have ever met that could neither read nor write; he had a number of dragon tattoos on his body and was missing his two front teeth. Despite his diminutive stature, he painted a sinister figure.

What I didn't know, was that he didn't know that GBH was his nickname...

Miners going off shift report to their shift boss, informing him what they have achieved on the completed shift and requesting supplies and equipment for the oncoming shift. One day, early on in my full-time shift boss role, I needed to get a jackhammer, air leg, three new drill steels and six bits down to GBH, for a new raise we were about to start on 11 level.

The crews had already gone underground and I wandered over to the stores to put my orders in. Without thinking too much about it, I pulled my materials from the stores and labelled up the new raise equipment with tags, writing "11 level GBH" so the banksman knew to which station to deliver the equipment. The banksman managed the bank which is the surface area around the head gear. Not to be confused with the place that extracts usurious amounts of your cash from you every time you have a bit of a night out just before payday. The banksman was the person who controlled and supervised movement of people and material to and from the surface to stations underground. A bit later in the morning I took the cage underground and started my rounds. It took some time to get to GBH's work area, and I arrived around crib time when the miners take a mid-shift break for something to eat and a cup of tea.

"Wasson?" I asked.

"Oh, she'll be right," he said. He chewed on his pasty thoughtfully. I waited for more information. I know better than to interrupt a Cornishman mid-pasty. "Why do you call me GBH then?" he eventually asked. That caught me off-guard as I realised that he hadn't known what we called him in management. This could become complicated. Probably the best way out of this sticky situation was to confess with the truth. I explained there was an understanding that he'd been inside for a while for grievous bodily harm. He continued munching, contemplatively, on his pasty but said no more. After his fuel ontake, we visited his work areas, inspected the ground conditions and discussed the plans. I thanked him and swiftly left to visit my next crew's workplace thinking to myself, "Wow, I got away with that."

On the next day, things seemed to go without a hitch at shift change. I started my rounds and got to GBH's crib box at mid-shift again.

"Wasson?" I started.

"Radon," he replied, munching sardonically. Then a minute later, "'Ere, Jack," he said, "I'd like you to call me AM from now on." I thought about this for a couple of seconds. I couldn't for the life of me think why he would ask this. His real name was Trevor.

He sat munching his pasty, looking at me from under his droopy lids. I sat and watched him, waiting for the explanation. He put down his pasty and I gulped as I realized he was readying himself for action. He has that focused look of a cat and seemed to be wiggling his arse ever so slightly. GBH suddenly leapt across the table, grasping me by the throat with his strong calloused hands, his fingers tightening on my scrawny neck. We rolled around in the mud like demented mud-wrestling seals. I felt the air slowly being choked out of me from the terrifying chokehold of an enraged Cornish nutcase. "It's Attempted Murder," he shouted into my face. Then, just as suddenly, he let me go amid peals of hysterical laughter echoing down the tunnels. Oddly enough, we became good pals after this. I had somehow passed a bizarre induction test thereby being admitted to the exclusive 'Mates of GBH' club.

Chapter 12: Students of My Own

"EDUCATION, n. That which discloses to the wise and disguises from the foolish their lack of understanding." – Ambrose Bierce, The Devil's Dictionary

One of the great joys of being part of an operating mine is the fun you can have at the expense of the mining-school students that come for work experience every summer. There is surely nothing more entertaining than testing the real-world knowledge of the hitherto academic engineer. Every year, the Cornish miners would contend with each other to test these earnest young learners.

During my first year as a full-time shift boss, two such students arrived in shiny new overalls and hard hats at the shift-boss office. I allocated one to Reggie Tellum's mining crew and the other to John Bolitho's. John was another good leading hand, who was mining a stope. They were told to shadow these teams, not to touch anything unless under supervision, but to make themselves helpful. They really couldn't do much with their lily-white hands and spindly arms and legs, but I thought they might learn something by observing the pros going about their daily business. The best miners are highly organised, and smart about scheduling tasks to minimise waiting time. The key is to ensure that a mining face is always available to drill. Miners make bonuses from the number of metres advanced or tonnes of ore blasted, often doubling or trebling their basic pay. Needless to say, it doesn't pay to get in their way.

On my regular rounds on that first student day, I arrived at Reggie Tellum's development ends. I found Reggie and his offsider drilling an end in their usual superlative way, but there was no sign of the student.

"OK, Reggie, where is he?"

"He'll be back dreckly."

"Oh aye?" I enquired.

"He's on a bleddy mission." Here we go. Clearly Reggie had sent him off to do something to get him out of the way.

"Where's he to?"

"He's to the stores, me 'ansome."

Despite my probing questions, it was obvious I wasn't going to get a straight answer from Reggie. He had those twinkling, mischievous blue eyes that many Cornishmen have, and everything told me that some tomfoolery was afoot.

Next I arrived at John Bolitho's stope. He too was drilling away with his offsider, and a similar discourse ensued in which it rapidly transpired that his student had also been sent off to the stores. I was in no doubt that they had thought up some ruse together. I finished my rounds and returned to the surface, determined to get to the bottom of the story. Entering the stores, I saw both students standing glumly by the counter, twiddling their thumbs.

"Right then, what are you up here for?" I demanded of the nearest one, "trying to get a suntan?"

"Sir, I've been sent up here to get a long weight." He said. Not the sharpest tool in the box.

"And you?"

"Me, sir? I've been sent for a tin of striped paint. They seem to be taking their time finding it!"

"And no doubt a tin of elbow grease," I said.

"How did you know?"

Cornish humour had duped the green students yet again. Indeed, the miner's ability for practical jokes is boundless, and new bloods are always easy pickings. Maybe too easy.

During this time, a good friend of mine was a presenter on BBC Radio Cornwall. One March evening, over a late dinner, we decided to play a practical joke on the listeners. On April 1st, I would ring in live on the show as Professor Stitchup of the Camborne School of Mines. The call went something like this:

"Is that Professor Stitchup on the line?" my presenter friend asked.

"Yes, that's me, dear. I have some very interesting news for your listeners. We have been studying the Chandler Wobble here at the School of Mines for quite some time, and it's getting a lot more wobbly."

"What exactly is the Chandler Wobble?"

"Well, I am glad you asked me that. The Chandler Wobble is the change in the spin of the Earth on its axis.

Think of the wobble you see in a toy top as it slows down. The top and the bottom of the top move erratically, like a sailor on the way to his longboat in Falmouth Harbour. The displacement of the Chandler Wobble is measurable. Imagine a gigantic pencil poked through the centre of the earth from the North to the South Poles. If that pencil tip was resting on a giant and very firm sketchbook, it would draw a circular path, not a dot, because of the wobble in the Earth's rotation. The existence of Earth's free nutation was predicted by Isaac Newton in Corollaries 20 to 22 of Proposition 66, Book 1 of the *Philosophiæ Naturalis Principia Mathematica*, and by Leonard Euler in 1765 as part of his studies of the dynamics of rotating bodies. The full explanation for the wobble involves the fluid nature of the Earth's outer core and oceans. The wobble, in fact, produces a very small ocean tide with an amplitude of approximately six millimetres, the so-called 'pole tide', which is the only tide not caused by an extra-terrestrial body."

"And for those of us who don't talk science twaddle?" she said.

"Let me try to simplify it for you. The Earth's North and South Poles are not always in the same place. What this means today is that Land's End is no longer the most westerly point in Britain, and it's now Cape Cornwall. We are going to have to rewrite all the guidebooks," I intoned scientifically.

We opened the lines and received hundreds of calls, including from Cornwall County Council. Even though we confessed at the end of the show that it was all an April Fools' hoax, BBC Cornwall went on receiving calls for months afterwards from concerned residents. Incidentally, the Chandler Wobble really does exist, trust me – or look it up on Wickedpedia.

On the next year's April 1st, we did a similar piece with Professor Stitchup. I then declared that, due to the extra weight of summer tourists at Land's End, the country had tilted slightly. The excessive number of visitors from the previous summer had added enough weight to exceed Young's modulus of elasticity of the Earth's crust and it wouldn't tilt back. I explained that, as a result, all of the canals running westwards were tilting downhill, and that barges were now travelling much faster in a westerly direction down the slightly inclined 'water slides'. It was much slower heading east, fighting against the current, and people in London would have to wait for their clotted cream.

It's fair to say that I would probably still be doing Professor Stitchup April Fools' pranks in Cornwall today had economic events not overtaken me. The International Tin Council had for years been propping up the price of tin by intervening in the market to buy spare metal capacity and store it in enormous warehouses. Like all market manipulations, though, this could not continue forever. By keeping the price of tin artificially high, more and more producers entered the market and the stockpile grew and grew. Eventually, like Camborne engineers on a bender, they ran out of money and it all ended in misery at the kebab shop, where there wasn't enough money to feed the partygoers. People were going to go kebab-less – the coffers were empty. The price of tin dropped from US$13,000 to US$3,000 per tonne almost overnight. The Wheal Jane mine which pumped about fifteen cubic metres of water for every tonne of ore hoisted went under. We marched in protest on London and fought to keep our mine afloat, but sadly, the Cornish mines floundered to an unhappy end; the red river stopped discharging its red plume into St Ives bay, and a thousand years of mining history closed its doors on the tough breed of Cornish miners. It was a sad day when the mines closed in Cornwall, one that would forever leave a scar in my mind. Those hard men did not deserve to have their livelihoods sacrificed at the altar of greed and power worshipped by the fat-cat bankers in the City. Our miners were ultimately victims of the failures of those apparently so much smarter than them. That's capitalism for you. Ironically, the red river was stained by the effluent from South Crofty mine near Camborne. Wheal Jane, the mine I had worked on, filled up with water once closed, and discharged its yellow ochre stained water into Falmouth bay, causing a furore by staining the hulls of the sailing boats of the bankers. Bankers, I said.

Anyway, personally tough decisions needed to be made - moving from one side of the sphere to the other is difficult at the best of times. However, by this stage in the narrative, I probably should have mentioned that I had got hitched to a lovely lady who was also working in Cornwall. She had built up a coterie of good friends, and her career was starting to blossom, so the decision was doubly difficult. My wife graciously allowed us to up sticks and emigrate to a country where mining is a national obsession, along with rugby, beer and going walkabout. What could possibly go wrong?

Chapter 13: The Australian Lead, Zinc and Copper Mines

"There is nothing more Australian than to spend time in someone else's country." – Unknown

When you move to a new country, it is always considered advisable to speak some of the local lingo. Of course, unlike French, Australian is a far easier than English, having dumbed itself down since leaving the motherland by ship. To speak Australian, you just add an 'o' as a suffix to any masculine word you can shorten. You add 'ie' or 'y' (pronounced 'e') in the case of the feminine words. Australians, like the French, give all sorts of stuff a gender.

For example, a break when you smoke is a "smoko." Someone who collects garbage is a "garbo." The word "afternoon", with three syllables, just doesn't stand a chance: it's devolved to "arvo." There are dozens of these masculine words, which you can try and work out for yourself: agro, alco, ambo, avo, biffo, compo, defo, dero, devo, doco, hospo, journo, mo, muso, milko, peto, povvo, rego, relo, reno, roo, servo, typo and vego. There are many more.

Feminine words include "Aussie" for Australian, "U-ey" for a U-turn, "dunny" for toilet, "beauty" for excellent and, of course, "barbie" for barbeque. A short list of feminine words might be: bikkie, brekkie, brickie, brumbie, billy, bikies, bevvy, biggie, bookie, blowie, Brissie, budgie (smugglers), Chrissie, chippy, chewy, choccy, cossie, ciggie, cluey, dunny, dodgy, exy, esky, furphy, footy, iffy, lanky, lippy, lolly, mossie, mushie, polly, pozzy, pressie, seppie, sunnies, sketchy, stubbie, tinnie, tradie, undies and veggie, to name but a few.

The list of specifically Aussie words is therefore enormous and, I submit, has been genderised. You heard it here first.

I was one of the lucky ones in the demise of the Cornish tin industry. With a certificate indicating something of an education, alongside some knowledge and experience, a large mining operation in Australia willingly sponsored me to join the company. With two pasties and a packet of ginger nuts in my pockets, I set off to the other side of the planet, to Mount Isa Mines, one of the biggest and most impressive underground rock factories in the world. Whilst I will never forget my fun days as a miner and shift boss in Cornwall and South Africa, the Isa, as it's often known, was to give me a real grounding as a mining engineer and allow me to experience the challenges of greater responsibility and way more sleepless nights.

Arriving at Isa for the first time leaves an impression. It's a mining town of 25,000 souls; it produces ten million tonnes of ore-bearing rock every year and is also a hotbed of engineering and safety excellence. The Isa was discovered in 1923 by Sir John Campbell Miles. It still produces thousands of tonnes of lead, silver and copper annually. It wasn't all peaches and roses, of course. The temperature was regularly over 45°C (113°F for the metrically challenged) for months at a time, and the flies would do anything to suck the salt and moisture out of you. I swear they have teeth. Later on, my mate Richard and I were to write a song about it. While I don't want to give away the story yet to come, the song does give a reasonable vignette of this oasis in the Aussie outback. The song was a rap song an went something like this:

Way back in 1923,
John Campbell Miles and his pony
Were rapping in the river, John turned and said
"Well, bugger me – I've discovered lead."

The place was hot, the flies were huge,
But John didn't mind, he'd got nothing to lose
So Campbell Miles, not being any wiser
Went and called the place 'Mount Isa'.

As time went by, the mine expanded,
The diggers and the riggers were all short-handed,
People came from all around,
To get down and dig it in that hole in the ground.

In years to come, I dare to say,
Everyone will live the Isa way,
This greenhouse thing is not absurd,
It's gonna get hot all over the world,

To give their gardens lots of water,
People used more hoses than they oughta,
They rolled them up down in the mine,
And put them in their ports on overtime.

They built a dam out at Moondara,
Pumped it up, but there was never any water,
They had to build one more again,
They forgot one thing – there was never any rain.

The work is good, the perks are great,
You can almost get anything past the gate,
And that's why Isa is the place to be,
You get yer money for nothing and yer parts for free.

Yes, they'll build a stack in every town,
And we'll all be diggers and we'll all get down
And that's why Isa is the place for me
You get yer money for nothing, and yer parts for free.

As a large mining town, the Isa contained all the flotsam and jetsam characters that populate such places. It was therefore close to a paradise for the nascent career of a young engineer. At first, I was shocked to hear people say that in the Isa there was everything you would ever need – clearly there was something in the water that was affecting peoples' brains.

Shortly after I arrived, I was followed by another mining engineer from Cornwall, Gutty Gilbert and his wife, Debbie. Gutty was the son of Ken Gilbert, the General Manager of Geevor, another of the Cornish tin mines that had perished as a result of the tin crisis. Gutty had also attained his qualification at Camborne School of Mines and was therefore a sound chap. Debbie had attained her qualification as a hairdresser at the technical college next door to the School of Mines. She quickly found a job as a hairdresser, and the North West Star (fondly referred to as the Nowhere Steer) ran a full-page ad for the Isa's new hairdresser, with her photo in full technicolour. 'Debbie Gilbert, direct from London.' Technically correct, but it does illustrate the hubris of the place, given that Debbie's first foray out of Cornwall was to catch the plane to the Isa, and Heathrow was as close as she had ever been to the capital.

My first foreman in the Isa was of German origin. Frans Bollmann was a neat man who enjoyed fermented cabbage and wearing lederhosen. He ran his crew with a ruthless military efficiency, with every rule and regulation followed to the letter. With his thick accent and love of regulations, the Isa's rumour mill suggested he was laying low, having escaped Germany on one of the ratlines of the Hitler youth. My impression of Frans was that he was a highly productive foreman who ran his area with great discipline, and a thick smattering of the dry German humour alluded to earlier.

Mount Isa Mines, like most large mining organisations, took more than its fair share of vacation students. It needs to be stated, if it's not immediately obvious, that this brings no immediate benefit to mining operations, since most students were about as much use as chocolate fireguards. The additional complication for Mount Isa was that, under Australian law, they had to take students from any discipline, not just a mining-related one. Usually, that didn't matter since Mount Isa is not the tourist destination a chat with the locals might lead you to believe. Even in the Tourist Information shop, they sell T-shirts showing a distant image of the copper stacks with the slogan "Happiness is Mount Isa... in your rear-view mirror." Indeed, from a satellite perspective, the Australian landmass looks like a vast pair of orangey-pink coloured buttocks, with Mount Isa, the brown-stained arsehole in the middle.

As a result, students who applied for work experience at Mount Isa tended to study mechanical engineering, geology, mining, or mineral processing. These budding troglodytes were marginally less incompetent than the rest of their university colleagues, and on one occasion, the ever-present rumour mill would have you believe, had actually been productive. This wasn't the case the year I arrived. After we had seen the dayshift miners off underground, the students trooped into the foreman's office. They lined up expectantly on one side of the room, shift bosses on the other. Frans, striding into the middle of the room, ramrod straight, all fire and brimstone, gave them his usual welcoming speech.

"You are the most useless bunch of fresh-air thieves it's been my unfortunate luck to clap eyes on. You will shortly go underground to see real men do real jobs with real big Tonka toys. You will not touch anything, you will not say anything, and you will under no circumstances do anything that puts people's lives at risk. Do you understand me?"

"Yes, sir."

"Did I ask you to speak? No. That is what is known as a rhetorical question. It seems they aren't teaching you much at your places of academic worship, certainly not the Kveen's English." I noticed a couple of tics in the jaws of the gaggle of shift bosses as they struggled with their internal clowns. One of them had an urgent need to leave the room. He missed the best bits.

"When I say jump, you say, 'How high?' When I say shit, you say, 'What colour?' And if you don't understand the question, which will be most of the time, you say, 'Do you want fries with that, sir?' Is. That. Clear?"

He stood daring the assembled student body to respond with his gimlet eyes.

"Think of it as practice for your future careers. If you step out of line, even a millimetre, you will find my boot so far up your arse your breath will smell of Kiwi. Do you understand me?"

Deafening silence.

Frans stalked down the line, asking each student their name and what mining discipline they were studying. He then either allocated the student to one of the shift bosses or sent them off to the mineral processing plant. He zeroed in on a gangly, spotty youth who declared, "Call me Cuthbert." The hairs on the back of Frans Bollmann's neck were starting to quiver. The expectant gaggle, already hushed, fell silent. All that could be heard was the faint hum of the overhead fans.

"And what do you do, Cuthbert?"

"I'm studying dentistry."

You could have heard a paperclip drop. Frans' face turned purple and the veins on his neck started to pulsate far more quickly than can be good for a man of his age.

"You," he said with an ominous growl, "will report to the 21-level maintenance shop, where you will put new teeth on loader buckets. Squad dismissed." A dam of suppressed honking exploded into the silence as the hooting gaggle bustled out, faster than fat kids chasing an ice-cream truck.

Chapter 14: All the World's a Stage

"The theatre, when all is said and done, is not life in miniature, but life enormously magnified, life hideously exaggerated." – H. L. Mencken

Life in a mining town wasn't all metal production and booze-ups. I have, in this telling of the story, deliberately avoided mention of the good women and children in my life so they can continue their existences untainted, so to speak, in the unlikely event that these tales were to be published.

The mining industry is tough on long-distance relationships, and I think my first marriage fell apart later on in my career because my first wife wanted a stable home base, whilst I have always had the gipsy gene and a love of travel. After all, it's hard to shoot a moving target.

One of the other loves in my life has been the theatre. When I arrived in Mount Isa, I immediately signed up to the Amateur Dramatics Society. I became involved in a number of shows: "Educating Rita," by Willy Russell, "Can't Pay, Won't Pay," by Dario Fo and "Waiting for Godot," by Samuel Beckett. I realise I may start to lose some of my mining readers' interest here, but hang in there - this does come back to mining.

One day the theatre group was called together for a meeting. We had been asked to put on a thirty-minute show for a gala dinner; the Institute of Engineers of Australia was planning its annual meeting in Mount Isa. The chairman of the Society thought it would be a good idea if we were to put on a comedy revue. This idea was enthusiastically embraced by the twenty or so members gathered. It was agreed we would all write a two or three-minute sketch and meet up the following week to consider what we had come up with. The next week's meeting was painful. Writing comedy is a serious business and, without wishing to blow my own horn (something I have always wanted to do but I regrettably lack both the needed length and flexibility), it rapidly became apparent that a guy called Richard Smallbone and I were the only ones with the slightest clue. It didn't take too long before Richard and I seized the process of writing the material, to the immense relief of the other eighteen stalwarts.

What ensued was a regular Smallbone/Shaft get-together a couple of nights a week. This usually entailed us getting regally sloshed and throwing comic ideas about, laughing deep into the night. Often we were too shit-faced – and consequently 'rufazrats', or in Australian, 'dusty' – to write down or even recall what we had earlier thought up, but over the ensuing months we managed to pull together a comedy revue that went down like a cold beer at a hot footy match. A well-fed and well-oiled audience in outback Australia in those days of limited TV and no internet proved a receptive crowd.

Given that we satirised the mining town itself, senior management and the people of Mount Isa, we were lucky to get away with it, although I suspect that if either of us had remained in Mount Isa for a lengthier period, there may have been more than just one rock ceiling above our heads. The script for our show has long been lost in the mists of time, but even now, thirty years later, I still recall a few of the sketches and songs we came up with. Please bear in mind that this was a performance for the Institute of Engineers, so we aimed to include some mildly technical humour. Funny or not? You decide.

The Engineers' Marriage Ceremony Sketch

"Dearly beloved. We are gathered here today for a double marriage ceremony; we will join this nut and this bolt, as well as this graduate mining engineer and this large mining company, into states of union.

Mechanics here present please note that construction is a true act of craftsmanship and, as such, should not be entered into lightly. Be there any man, or woman, or transgender individual, who believes that the threads will not match, let him, or her, or him-her, speak now or forever retool his jig.

Do you, 45 mm slot-headed ABS number 077871 dynamic tension bolt, take this nut to be your permanently attached coupling, to secure and to anchor, to hold and to harness, in lubrication and in dry fit... until a hacksaw do you part?

Do you, 60 mm cross-section, course-threaded ABS number 96425 security locking nut, take this bolt to be your lawfully attached tether, to grip and to clasp, to have and to hold, in tension or in compression, within the elastic limits... until breaking strain do you part?

Do you have the washer?

I now pronounce you, well and truly... cross-threaded."

"Now, graduate mining engineer and large company, which shall remain anonymous; employment is a wage-earning experience which should be taken seriously. Be there anyone here present who believes that the job interview was of any use whatsoever, let him speak now and be retrenched.

Do you, young, eager, but basically useless graduate mining engineer, take Mount Isa M..., this mining company, to be your lawful employer? To serve and to service, to fudge and to bludgeon, on staff and on award, until a manager's ticket and better job do you part?

Do you, bloated, obdurate, bureaucratic mining company, take this engineer to be your long-term employee? To befuddle and bullshit, to hire and fire, without why or wherefore, until a falling copper price or depleted ore reserve do you part?

Do we have the housing loan?

Graduate mining engineer, and Mount... large mining company. I pronounce you well and truly engaged... at least temporarily."

Of course, nothing rounds off a show better than a rousing finale song full of vim and vigour. However, I do need to preface this song with a short story. The ladies of Mount Isa were limited in number in comparison with the men, it being a mining town after all. This meant that there was an enormous amount of unconstrained testosterone around, which made the place an ideal hunting ground for ladies looking for... fun.

As often as not, the ladies of the town, not feeling any need to compete, were generally somewhat larger than the average female circumference. Now, I have always been a man who likes a bit of something to grab onto, so I do not mean this to be critical; after all, this fits with the family motto, "The more the merrier", which is applied to all the important facets of life; the fairer sex, drugs and rock 'n' roll.

There was one particular lady amongst the Isa gems who was superior in every way. She was a schoolteacher of comforting proportions who liked to dress in black, and who, as a result, was fondly if somewhat uncharitably referred to as, 'the Hearse'. She also had a voracious appetite for men, and could fairly be described as a cougar It seems unfair to me that if a man has a number of partners he is thought a stud, whereas a woman is usually thought of far more pejoratively as a slut. I therefore submit that, in Australia, the man should be termed a 'studdo', and the women a 'studdie'. What do you think?

The Hearse had added a good few notches to her bedposts as she studied her way round the bars of the town. Among the bachelor element of Isa society, it was not regarded as a medal of distinction to be known as the cause one of those notches.

One evening, Smallbone had chatted her up in the Irish Club and arranged a secret assignation; nobody knew anything about this. He would have certainly taken this secret to the grave, except for one minor inconvenience. When the Hearse left Mount Isa, she took out a full-page advert in the Northwest Star, naming every person she had slept with, and grading them out of ten. I guess school-teacherly ways run deep. To Smallbone's immense shame, he came in (if you will excuse the phrase) second from last with the pitiful score of one and a half. Whether he got these points for degree of difficulty, timing, or persistent faulting is unknown. He then became the butt of many a joke for a long time after that, and I suspect that it was this incident, more than any other, that drove him to leave the mines and pursue a different livelihood. Clearly, this had not been his best performance.

To give him his due, he did see the funny side, and this experience became the basis for the song we later wrote, celebrating the larger ladies of the town. This was the song that was to close our comic revue, to be sung the tune of the traditional Irish folk song, 'Molly Malone'.

The Mount Isa Anthem

In Cholesterol City, the girls are so pretty,
They trundle their way through the heart-attack zone.
With cheeks broad and sallow, and arteries narrow,
They will not much longer be alive, alive–o.
Alive, alive–o–o; alive, alive–o–o,
They will not much longer be alive, alive–o.

She once had a murmur, and sure t'was no wonder,
For mother and father were both fatties too.
To speed up reduction, she underwent suction,
And the fat it came out in great globs, a–globs–o.
Great globs, a–globs–o–o, great globs, a–globs–o–o,
The fat it came out in great globs, a–globs–o.

The doctor was tired, the machine was mis-wired,
Instead of with suction it started to blow.

With one final shudder, she succumbed to the blubber,

      Reached critical mass to explode, explode–o.
      Explode, explode–o–o, explode, explode–o–o,
      Reached critical mass to explode, explode–o.

      The size of the coffin, they carried her off in,
      Was larger by far than the average box.
      And the hole in the ground, where her bones can be found,

      Is six long and six deep and six wide, a–wide–o,
      Six wide, a–wide–o–o, six wide, a–wide–o–o
      six long and six deep and six wide, a–wide–o.

I, of course, being married, was not subject to such shenanigans. My wife and I had managed to conceive our first child in the Isa. Our daughter had in fact been somewhat reluctant to enter the world and, considering where we were living, I felt this was completely understandable. At seventeen days overdue, and with a head the size of a bowling ball according to the scan, my long-suffering wife was starting to get concerned about expelling this bundle of joy. We had tried all sorts of methods to encourage world entry - the Greek induction method, the French induction method... but in the end the Aussie induction method did the trick. In a less than clairvoyant planning move, having just done a 'doublo' underground (two eight-hour shifts back to back), my wife persuaded me that a trip down the twenty-mile corrugated dirt track to Rifle Creek Dam might do the trick.

For those who haven't ridden dirt roads in the outback, after being graded flat, over a period of months and years, the track develops small waves of corrugation about 50 cm apart with troughs about 20 cm deep between them. If you get the speed of your vehicle just right you can skim across these like a hovercraft, but if you don't, you bounce around like a tennis ball being prepared for service at Wimbledon, smashing your skull on the roof of the vehicle and permanently removing a few more grey cells residing within.

On the way back from this adventure, my wife informed me that the pool of liquid building up on the floor pan of our old Land Cruiser was not the aircon leaking but was due to the fact that her waters had broken. My firstborn child arrived fifteen minutes after we got back to town, to the immense joy of all our overseas family.

The Isa wasn't all wine, women and song. As an engineer gaining experience, I started to climb the greasy pole of responsibility. After shift bossing for a while, I became the mine equipment engineer responsible for buying all the big drilling machines, trucks and other mobile equipment. I then became relief foreman at Hilton mine, and blasting engineer. The Isa was a fantastic place to hone mining and management skills, and after nearly five years, I had finally achieved a position of some significance as an underground manager.

Of course, in the Isa, we took consultation with the workforce incredibly seriously; teamwork, bottom-up planning, six sick notes, employee consultation and participation, the works. Hearing what our people were saying was an essential part of the planning process, officially, but here is how it pans out in reality.

The Plan – Shit Happens

In the beginning there was the Plan.

Then came the Assumptions.

And the Assumptions were without form.

And the Plan was without substance.

And darkness was upon the face of the Miners.

And the Miners spoke amongst themselves saying, "This is a bucket of shit and it bloody stinks."

The Miners went unto their Shift Boss, saying unto him, "It is a pail of dung and we can't live with the smell."

The Shift Boss went unto his Foreman, saying, "It is a container of excrement so strong, such that none may stomach its odour."

The Foreman went unto the Mine Manager, saying, "It is a vessel of fertilizer and none may abide its strength."

The Mine Manager spoke with the other General Managers, saying, "It contains that which aids plant growth and it is very strong."

The General Manager went unto the Directors, saying, "It promotes growth and it is very powerful."

The Directors went unto the CEO, saying unto him, "This new Plan will actively promote the growth and vigour of the company with very powerful effects."
The CEO looked upon the Plan and saw that it was good.
And the Plan became policy.

And that, my friends, is how shit happens.

Chapter 15: Steamy Revelations

"May the roof above you never fall in and those gathered beneath it never fall out." – Ancient Irish toast.

By this time, I had attained Australian citizenship for they no longer required a criminal record. I had also slowly become a big fish in a small pond having attained the dizzying heights of underground manager. Living proof, I feel, that if you hang around long enough somewhere, just like a turd in a cesspool, you will eventually float to the top. I started to hear myself thinking, "You know there is everything you need at the Isa, why would you want to live anywhere else?"

This state of nirvanic bliss didn't last forever. Firstly, there was a trip to visit Kiruna mine in Sweden to investigate automated in the hole hammer drilling and driverless trains, which now sound pretty lame by today's AI standards. Thirty years ago it was incredible and opened my eyes to a place where new innovations were happening every week, where the world reminded you that you were alive by the sting of cold rain on your face, and where open-mindedness about the rest of the world was a way of life.

This different approach to things can be well demonstrated by my experience the evening I arrived in Kiruna. Checking in to the hotel, the desk clerk, as she gave me the key to my room, asked if I would like a relaxing sauna before dinner. This sounded like a splendid idea to the weary traveller, and she kindly indicated the route to the sauna. Being a reticent, retiring, reserved Englishman, I donned my budgie smugglers and wrapped the voluminous white hotel towel around my midriff. I navigated the corridor to the sauna room and opened the door.

A wave of steaming hot air hit me and, as the haze cleared, I blinked in amazement. Before me was a small room full of naked Swedes of both the male and female varieties. Nothing was left to the imagination. I was clearly overdressed. I hesitated. I could retreat now and forever condemn the British nation to a reputation for prudishness in the minds of these beauteous blonde bombshells, or I could enter the steaming cabin and play the ignorant foreigner. I plumped for the latter, placing myself on a low seat next to the wall at the end furthest from the hot stones. Neatly placing the folded towel on the bench, I kept my eyes steadfastly on the stones trying to appear indifferent. I certainly did not want to be eyeballing any of the breasts swinging a few sweaty inches from my perspiring face. Just as I thought that I had managed to avoid any eye contact with the assembled naked host, an ageing Scandi-hooligan got up and walked down the line to stand directly in front of me. He lifted one of his legs onto my bench, giving me a full sausage-and-plums eyeful. I looked up into his laconic grin.

"Why are you wearing your pyjamas in the sauna?", he asked gently.

I stood up and slowly dropped my trunks, as the entire group looked on, no doubt giving me grades for skill, style and size; one of the more embarrassing moments of my life (so far, at least). Now, whenever I have to give a public speech of some sort, I think back to that moment and say to myself, "How bad can it possibly get?" I nearly always come back with the thought... "Not THAT bad."

The second pin in my balloon of paradisiacal Mount Isan whimsy came during my fifth year at the Isa when I had my routine annual review. The HR guy asked me the usual drivel: "What do you regard as your greatest weakness?." I always think you can answer this in one of two ways and neither of them is a win. You can take the honest, humble route, and provide an actual weakness, or you can spew some drivel about a great weakness that is actually a strength. Either way, the point of the question is to uncover some sort of fault. Either real as you confess to some inherent personality flaw, or you give evidence of your enormous bullshitting ability. I gave him some BS about being a perfectionist and having to make sure that everything I was involved in was as good as it could possibly be, rather than just good enough. Yawn.

Then the next routine question, "Where do you see yourself in five years' time?" Another question to which there is no right answer. Either you come across as overly pushy, self-assured and with naked ambition to the point of arrogance, or you can be seen as having no drive. I was beginning to tire of the whole pointless process, and nakedness, both metaphorical and real, was starting to become a habit.

"Tell you what," I said, "why don't you tell me where you think I could be in five years' time?"

He was a little taken aback. He thought for a few seconds and then launched into, "Well, you could be underground manager on the copper section, or underground manager of the lead section, or..." Yawn. None of it was inspiring; basically, I would be exactly where I was now, just doing it in a different area of the mine.

"Thanks," I mumbled, with as much enthusiasm as I could muster. We meandered to the end of this painful process, and I then got up to leave. I had pretty much decided that the next five-year scenario presented was not for me.

As I got to the door, I turned and said, "I've got another question for you. If I was travelling in a car with you at the speed of light and you turned the lights on, what would happen?"

He looked at me with that blank, flummoxed expression you see when someone is drinking something as pointless as decaffeinated coffee, or alcohol-free beer.

"Yep – some questions don't have a right answer," I said as I shut the door.

Career-limiting for sure, but then the career he was describing wasn't the one I wanted, and it was time to move on to greener pastures. Indeed, with Mount Isa being in the middle of the dusty outback, it was as brown and red as you were likely to get. Anywhere would be greener than this.

I decided to look for an opportunity to change career, which is no easy thing in the middle of a recession. The benefit of being in a vocational career becomes a ball and chain when you decide to move into something else: your skills as a miner are not that transferrable. After all, shovelling shit and blowing things up are not required that often in the corporate world. Or maybe they are?

I managed to persuade the Cranfield School of Management into letting me join their one-year MBA programme. I can only surmise that I may have represented a management-level window into the real world of blood, sweat and tears. They told me that I could shed light on the heavy industrial mining world to other students. Perhaps they just wanted me to clean the lecture-hall windows. I left the red-rust earth of the Isa for the leafy green of Bedfordshire, back in England, in the mistaken belief that this would lead me to a highly paid role. My initial desire to avoid desk work and live in the physical world had all but evaporated by this stage. Indeed, it was clear that the highest you could climb in an underground mine was the surface.

Chapter 16: Becoming an MBA, (Master of Bullshit, Arsehole)

"Don't sell the steak, sell the sizzle" – Elmer Wheeler
"No-one really wants a drill, they want a hole" – Jack Shaft

The School of Management proved a fascinating place for a mining engineer. Prior to this experience, I believed that you just dug stuff up, processed it into a useable, saleable product and then sold it on the market for the price of the day. I affectionately thought that this was how all businesses work. But no; I discovered, with incredulity, the power of marketing. The power of putting lipstick and fur on a pig to make it look like a cuddly, desirable alpaca. The amazing ability of people in the corporate world to bullshit about anything and everything, and to do so with a passion and fervour that would make Trump blush. I felt at home, at last, in a place where bullshit baffles brains.

If the Camborne School of Mines had been academically taxing (who, except for a PhD in physics, has any idea what the paradox of Schrödinger's cat is, or indeed why it might be important), the School of Management took a different approach. They overloaded you with so much work that it was nigh impossible to actually do it all as an individual. The immense workload taught students to harness the power of their study groups, to work in teams and to play to their own and other team members' strengths. Once formed, study groups typically went through three phases: storming, norming and performing.

Storming: the group argues about everything, like a bunch of two-year-olds fighting over a piece of chocolate cake.

Norming: the group appreciates each other's strengths. Every team needs a washer-upper for the coffee cups (one of my strengths).

Performing: the group learns to work together using each other's skills for the optimal and least time-consuming outcome.

It was a very useful experience that honed most of the students into powerful team players, and it helped me enormously in my later business life.

I met all sorts of people at the School of Management, many of whom were set on the path of entrepreneurial bliss. This inspired me to want to do my own thing one day. And one day I did... but that is for later chapters.

Some nascent entrepreneurs, like Pete Tiler, took spectacular steps - like cutting up their business suits or setting fire to them on Guy Fawkes Night. These suits, essential during their previous corporate lives, were demolished, symbolically closing the door on that life. I found that impressive, if a little intimidating. Pete came to regret this after the business school course was over, since nearly all entrepreneurs have to squeeze cash out of banks, and banks were pretty conservative. Pete, turning up in a T-shirt bearing the slogan, 'Revolt – not for Tossers' (advertising his brewery), was somewhat surprised to be shown the other side of the revolving door in short order.

There were of course some spectacularly bad business ideas. For example, selling pet rocks in cages (even a mining engineer knew that was pretty dumb). Condom key chains: prophylactics, sealed in plastic and attached to a keyring with a cheeky slogan: 'In Case of Emergency, Break Glass.' The Pissfit Club: A club dedicated to preparing members for marathon drinking sessions such as stag and hen parties.

Whilst most people in business school were staunch Conservatives, believing that taxes should be as low as possible to encourage new business, there was the occasional loony-left idea too. One such idea came from a guy called Tom, who later became a multibillion-pound company CEO, and who has latterly given large sums to the Labour Party. His idea for a political party was 'Scum be gone'. The idea was that anyone who took drugs should be given unlimited quantities of their drug of choice. The only catch was that they be castrated or neutered so they couldn't reproduce. A halfway house Darwin Award idea. Tom was pretty serious about this, and it just shows how effective the creative mind can be when faced with a particular social challenge. That Tom became such a socialist in middle age is something of an anathema. Perhaps one of his children took to drugs?

After the School of Management, I became increasingly desperate for gainful employment. Our second child was on the way, and a life of abject poverty in Milton Keynes did not seem very appealing. Just as I was about to throw in the towel and return to the Isa with my tail between my legs, a friend from my study group at Cranfield called me and asked if I was interested in a job at Siemens Telecoms. One that she had been offered but wouldn't take because it was too boring. She knew how to sell an idea and flatter an ego at the same time. Frankly, at this stage, I would have taken a job kissing arses at the doors of the Houses of Parliament. I happily took up the opportunity of interviewing for the role of Commercial Manager, Customer Services Division, thinking I was probably there to make up the interview numbers, and that the job was already slated for an internal candidate. It was, after all, a role for which I had absolutely no qualifications or experience whatsoever.

Chapter 17: Tele Cons

"When one door closes, another one opens." – Alexander Graham Bell

I was interviewed for the post on a Friday afternoon by the Finance and Commercial Director, Klaus Piltzoon, a German gentleman who had a cracking dry sense of humour. Given that my chances of getting this job were slightly lower than a snowball's chance in Hell, I relaxed into it. This proved to be the right approach. At the conclusion of the interview, he nodded at the HR director and then asked me, "So, ven can you start?"

"Monday," I said, tongue in cheek.

"Great. See you Monday, nine o'clock sharp."

And that was that. I had now joined the telecoms industry. It proved to be a fascinating job, which I immensely enjoyed for a couple of years. Given my dire financial situation at the time, it took me about six pay cheques to build up the courage to ask Klaus exactly why he thought it a good idea to employ me, given my paucity of either telecoms industry or customer service functional experience.

"Vel," he pondered, "Ve thought you had a good sense of humour and it would be funny to vork with you." Not quite the ringing endorsement I was hoping for, and to date, I have kept him off my CV as a reference.

I settled into the new role reasonably well. It was fun to work with telecoms engineers and salespeople - working out project profitability, ensuring those working for bonuses did not reduce prices so much that there was no room for profit and keeping an eye on the technical guys so they would not over-design or deliver additional and free work for their buddies in the client company. I oversaw a team of analysts doing contract value analysis, a team of invoice clerks, and a crew of credit controllers who chased overdue customers. The toughest element was dealing with my credit control department, who were mostly female, and mostly ferocious. In hindsight, I would far rather face a hundred and twenty kilos of angry rock driller than fifty kilos of slightly annoyed credit controller. Whilst the rock driller can be as physically intimidating as a riled-up alpha gorilla, the credit controller deploys sarcasm, cynicism and passive-aggression with the highly honed skills of a verbal samurai whilst eating glass sandwiches for lunch.

During this time, child number two was making his presence increasingly apparent in my wife's waistline. It is notable that child number one didn't show for about six months, and my wife maintained a svelte, slim-line figure during this whole time. Something to do with the integrity of the muscular structure of the female torso prior to any pregnancy, I am led to understand. However, once the full term of a pregnancy has been experienced, the second time around, muscle memory takes over and the belly basically flops out immediately following conception. Now, nine months later, the lad developing inside was showing a similar reluctance to our first lass to enter the oxygenated world. I knew better than to test the cobbled roads of rural Buckinghamshire and we decided to wait it out.

At last, it seemed the evening of impending arrival was upon us. Contractions were coming ninety seconds apart and my mother-in-law was looking after lass number one. Our 'birtho' bag was packed and in the metal chariot. We stumbled out to the car for the ten-mile ride to Milton Keynes hospital. It was ten p.m. when we set off. As we left, immediately the contractions stopped. Another three miles, still nothing. My wife was starting to feel quite chipper again; well, at least the cursing headed my way had reduced significantly. At mile five there was a modest kick from the incumbent, but still no contractions. I suggested to my wife that it would be nice to stop for a medicinal drop of the amber nectar in the White Hart at Newport Pagnell. To give her due respect, she did actually consider this suggestion, but we decided to soldier on to the hospital, just in case. And just as well. Once into the maternity section, the Irish charge nurse took one look at the business end and immediately went into overdrive, preparing my wife on the gurney.

"Yer feckin' twelve centimetres dilated, luv," she stated, matter-of-factly.

The baby was delivered three minutes later, emerging faster than a striking mamba. But for my wife's overriding sanity, the young lad would have been born in a pub. We decided to name him after a beer, and it has to be noted that he has always been extremely comfortable in clubs, pubs and bars: a chip off the old block... well, rock.

At one stage in my telecoms career, I needed to fill the customer services contact position for Ford of Europe. This was a huge account, as Siemens had fifty engineers on their sites around Europe. It was made doubly sensitive due to the fact that Ford had refused to sign our contractual terms and retained the right to terminate the contract at a month's notice. We couldn't afford to lose this valuable account. I therefore went about the interview process diligently. One potential account controller, Freddy Woodhead, was an internal candidate from our northern offices. He was a pretty laid-back bloke and walked into the interview sporting a ponytail, earrings, a woolly jumper and clogs. As a miner, I could just about see him walking into the change house dressed like this. As a customer services contact manager in a customer-facing role, it was a stretch.

I interviewed Freddy, carefully working through his experience, skills and training record. He was okay but needed more training in sales and effective communication. I thanked him for his time and told him I would let him know in relatively short order. At the end of the day, I reviewed the candidate with HR and decided not to take his application any further. We politely informed him by email.

The next day, as I was working through my incoming mail, Freddy called me. He wanted to know what he could do to improve his chances in the future. I, unsurprisingly, suggested a training course in sales skills and effective communication. He continued to badger me for other suggestions. Taking a deep breath, I suggested that he might like to think about how an account-facing executive should present himself from a sartorial perspective for a large account with a prestigious, corporate customer. He could perhaps dispense with the clogs and the earrings and consider a dark suit. I asked him to think about what such a customer would expect to see in their point of contact from an attire standpoint. He thanked me for my time.

Less than an hour later, Klaus appeared at my office door. I could tell that he was upset, the clues being the twitching muscles in his jaw, his puce red face and his deeply furrowed brow.

"Is it true that you told zis member of staff zat he should change his manner of dressing in order to get ze account position for Ford?", he enquired through clenched teeth.

"I actually told him he needed some self-development training, but I did mention a possible dress code. Do you think a guy who comes in wearing a woolly jumper, clogs, earrings and a ponytail would be okay for Ford?", I responded.

"Vell, no, ve cannot say zees things. It is not correct politically. You are not down ze pit now!" he shot back.

"Are not our Siemens values: Truth, Honesty..."

He uncharacteristically interrupted me. "Not zee point. You cannot do zees things. It is insupportable."

I maintained a respectful silence as he spun on his heels and stormed off. Strewth, now I am in trouble, I thought. About an hour later I received from HR a notice of the written warning for inappropriate behaviour with respect to management of staff. I cogitated this for a while and considered the hypocrisy of it all. It came as a surprise to me that we weren't living our values after all the training I had received in them.

The next day I tottered across the floor of my cubicle team and into my office. The usual hubbub slowly subsided, as thirty-six pairs of eyes lifted from their screens and locked on to this six-foot tower of queenly beauty. Finding size eleven black high heels and a black dress with a forty-inch chest size had been a mission, but with the lippy, makeup, eyelashes, short little black number, earrings and handbag, I could have easily given Tutu a run for his money, though I needed a little more practice with the walk. It's not easy walking on heels.

Someone had clearly let Klaus' secretary know for about a minute later Klaus again appeared at my door. I hadn't heard him swear before, but this day he closed the door and sized me up with a long stare. The silence extended for a good sixty seconds.

"You hef made your fucking point. Warning withdrawn. Go home now and change immediately."

We never spoke of it again, but I have this sense that he thought it quite amusing in his dry German way, and grudgingly gave a little more rope to his cross-dressing miner. I worked at Siemens Telecoms for three years and found it a satisfying experience.

Having spent the early years of my career going underground at the crack of sparrow fart, I continued to get up early in order to get the day going. One April 1st, I got into the office early and quickly went around the sales office with some clear Sellotape. The phones in those days were fixed line and had a sprung lever that rose when you lifted the handle to connect the call. I carefully taped all of these down. The sales team trooped in after their morning meeting just before eight o'clock, and the phones started to ring. They picked up the handles, but the phones just wouldn't connect, and all hell started breaking loose. Frustrated salespeople were throwing their toys out of the pram as they couldn't talk to the calling customers. I watched with huge amusement for a few minutes at which point someone spotted the tape and put them out of their misery. I am pretty sure Klaus worked out it was me, but he never asked, so the truth value wasn't tested again.

However, it was clear to me I was never going to get very far in Siemens given my lack of technical and functional training, and therefore I could expect to languish in a back room greyly preparing for retirement. Not for me, and the clarion call of the mining world was starting to amplify in my brain. I had a hankering to be back with the heady lunacy and the exposure to the nut-jobs and crazies; to feel again the sheer excitement of not knowing quite what would happen next.

I decided that a life in the City of London, in mining corporate finance, would be the ideal mix of the skills learned at Siemens and those in the mines. I fondly imagined that the City was full of merry bankers and analysts all chummily working together, throwing buckets of money about at whatever mining project took their fancy this week. Of course, I couldn't have been more wrong.

Chapter 18: Mine Banker

"Hospitals report that the hearts of bankers are in strong demand by transplant patients, because they've never been used." – Bankers Magazine 1920s

Once I had decided on this course, my first interview was with an American banker, owner and chairman of his own firm, The Dog Group. I was shown into his office by his secretary and was surprised to see an enormous pair of Texan boots atop the desk, attached to a portly form hidden behind a copy of the Sun newspaper. Red braces prevented his trousers from slipping to his ankles, and he wore a matching red bow tie. A shiny bald head sported John Lennon glasses, accentuating beady blue eyes. I thought I was about to hear that infamous Oxford interview line, "Impress me, boy," and I rustled around forlornly in my trousers looking for a lighter with which to set fire to his newspaper. No luck, but in any case, he laid down his paper and asked me the usual stuff. What do you know about the firm? Tell me about yourself. What are your strengths? What are your weaknesses? Nothing really to write home about. The interview went reasonably well. At the end, he stood up and rocked forward on the tips of his toes to attain his full height of 5 ft 2 in (157 cm). He pulled out his red braces to the full length of his arms and let them snap back to his chest and stomach with a resounding thwack.

"Are you hungry, boy?" he growled.

Mistakenly thinking this was an invitation to lunch, I replied politely, "Well, I am a little bit peckish."

His eyebrows beetled somewhat. I realised that this could lose me the job. I think he was trying to gauge whether I was taking the piss. He decided correctly that I wasn't and, with a few more formalities, I joined the company five weeks later having served out my notice with Siemens.

The City proved to be very different from my expectations. I joined at the tail end of what had been irrational exuberance in the mining sector. There were parties deep into the night funded by banks, there were long boozy lobster lunches, and there were lines of cocaine, the drug of choice for the yuppies that inhabited this den of demonic debauchery. I enjoyed these parties for a while as I was finding my feet, but then Bre-X happened.

Bre-X was the immovable Indonesian tree that fell across the motorway in front of the speeding mining investment juggernaut. That tree stopped the investment boom dead in its tracks and the juggernaut turned itself into a yard sale of epic proportions. It took a while - like watching a train wreck in slow motion. Small banks, brokers and investment funds closed shop, swathes of analysts and backroom boys were laid off; salespeople could not pay their car loans and were forced to return their Porsches and Ferraris. The lights went out.

Bre-X was the extraordinary story of a junior gold-mining company which 'discovered' the gold find of the century in Kalimantan, Indonesia. In 1996, Bre-X's share price peaked at $286.50 on the Toronto Stock Exchange, with a total capitalization of more than six billion dollars. The company claimed from its drilling results to control roughly eight percent of all of the world's known gold resource.

In December 1996, Lehman Brothers recommended a buy on 'the gold discovery of the century'. Major mining companies such as Barrick Gold, Placer Dome and Freeport-McMoRan Copper & Gold, among other top producers, fought an epic battle to get a piece of this impressive deposit. In the same year, Bre-X hit a snag with the Indonesian government, who claimed that Bre-X was not playing by the 'rules' of the country. Bre-X's exploration permits were revoked. Indonesia's Suharto regime expropriated forty percent of the deposit for Indonesian interests. Nationalization is nothing new in the mining sector, but this was pretty much gun-to-the-head diplomacy.

Then (surprise, surprise), just as people were beginning to ask more searching questions and due diligence was just getting going, in January 1997, a fire in Busang destroyed most of the sample records. Despite this act of nature, a joint venture was agreed that gave Indonesia a forty percent share, Bre-X forty-five percent and Freeport-McMoRan fifteen percent.

Fidelity Investments, Invesco Funds Group, and other mutual-fund companies piled into the stock. J.P.

Morgan bankers talked up the project in a conference call in which the project's top geologist predicted the deposit might contain a staggering 200 million ounces of gold, worth over $240 billion at the gold price of the day. One of Canada's top gold analysts said, "What most people are now realising is that this company has made one of the greatest gold discoveries ever." Irrational exuberance is a term that was perhaps conservatively applied to Bre-X.

However, as 1997 progressed, Freeport began due diligence on the deposit in earnest and several twin holes were drilled. What could possibly go wrong? Indeed, what quickly became apparent was that the gold in the Bre-X samples was alluvial gold, panned by local artisanal miners and bought by Guzman, the Bre-X geologist, to salt their samples. The gold in the samples had, for the most part, been fraudulently added, and the Freeport holes quickly confirmed the fraud of the century.

Guzman, on his way to meet with the Freeport geologist, surprisingly fell out of the helicopter he was travelling in, in an apparent suicide. Jungle pigs had eaten his face and hands in the three days it took to find him and, incredibly, it was not possible to definitively identify him. It is interesting to note that the body of a man of similar age had also just gone missing from the local morgue and was never seen again.

It was a story of death, intrigue, corruption and fraud. Did Guzman actually die? That is an open, conspiracy-theory question. Nobody knows, but South

America would be a good place to disappear with a large stash of ill-gotten gains.

On the plus side, this massive gold mining fraud, possibly the largest in history, gave impetus to CRISCO, an international group formed in 1994 to develop a code for mineral resource reporting; one that makes it much more difficult to tamper with results. The CRISCO code was adopted by the main international resource management bodies. This included a grouping of organisations that are responsible for developing mineral reporting codes and guidelines that covered more than 80 percent of the listed capital of the mining industry. In brief, the mining industry sorted its shit out.

However, the immediate effect of the Bre-X train crash was a precipitous drop in inward investment into mining's exploration sector. In the year prior to Bre-X, there had been roughly $34 billion flowing to support the exploration for, and the development of, new mines. The following year it had fallen to less than $1 billion, and much of this was the tail end of committed investment from before Bre-X.

The party was over. The City became more cut-throat. The long lunches disappeared. Parties were few and far between. The mining investment industry of which I was a part hunkered down. I spent a couple of years analysing potential investments for my boss, taking meetings with the guys he didn't want to see and with whom he would never invest, and looking for money for the projects that had his attention. He was a likeable fellow once you got to know him, though I did get fired about once every six months for some sin or another... usually when the boss and I were on the razz together. My approach was to sit at home the morning after. At about ten a.m. the phone would ring and, "Where the fuck are you?" would be bellowed through the earpiece.

"Well, you fired me last night, so I thought I had better get myself a new job."

"Get your arse into town right now. As you well know, anything said after three beers doesn't count." Everything would be hunky-dory for a few months until I did something else to displease His Eminence.

Chapter 19 – Doggy Style

"Some days you're the fire hydrant, and some days you're
the dog."
– Parker Conrad

The Dog Group owned projects and assets all over the developing world, known internally as Dog Projects. With the disappearance of inward investment, the company needed to keep me occupied. The ending of apartheid in South Africa and the fall of the Iron Curtain created many opportunities. The boss had snapped up some of these and I was sent on missions to resolve the inevitable problems. Not all sweets in the sweet shop are sweet.

One time, I went to South Africa and Lesotho; I called the mission, "Who let the dogs out?." Back in my old stomping ground, but with apartheid now gone, it was a very different place. One of my jobs was to staunch the loss of diamonds from the Messina and Star mines. Diamonds were running at thirty-six carats per hundred tonnes of ore at these mines. A carat is two grams; in essence the mine was running at seventy-two grams of diamond per hundred tonnes of material, or about three-quarters of a gram per tonne. A standard packet of sugar weighs a thousand grams. To put this into context, it's like looking for a packet of sugar in one thousand four hundred tonnes of rock, which in layman's terms, is thirty-five large truckloads. Quite difficult to spot and pinch you might think, but grade going in did not align with diamonds going out with the tailings, and those retained for sale by the mine. On average, the unaccounted diamonds comprised around ten percent, which was a large chunk of profit.

My job was to put a stop to the thefts by discovering how they did it, and then putting in place mechanisms to stop them doing it. As a youthful thirty-something, I clearly looked pretty green when I rocked up at the mine as the chairman's emissary.

Despite the politeness from the senior team – South Africans are zealously deferential to any position of authority – I could see they thought I was merely a dumb City suit. I would be nothing but an incumbrance and that I should be parked in a corner as quickly as possible so I wouldn't get in the way of the serious business of management and mining. I was happy to comply, deciding to apply a stealth approach to my mission. I was also happy not to disclose my previous mining experience in South Africa. Knowledge of the mining lingua franca, Fanakalo, could prove helpful when nobody knows you understand it. I kept a low profile.

I spent a few days walking the process from stope to shaft to plant, noting down potential areas of vulnerability and talking to people through the translator who had been thoughtfully provided. Sometimes it was hard not to butt in and say something when a faceworker or shift supervisor said something particularly interesting, but I managed not to give the game away; working through a translator gave me a little more time to think, analyse and plan my next question.

The translator would introduce me as the "spukapuk madoda" which I knew to mean 'stupid man'. He would then yak away about anything and everything. The translator and interviewee rarely actually talked about the question I asked, and the translator would then give me some benign factoid after a couple of minutes of conversation. He must have thought I was particularly stupid to think that it takes two minutes to answer a simple question. I let it ride as I was getting far more titbits listening to the real chats he was having. One thing that did confuse me in the plant was the regular mention of feeding the pigeons. I thought perhaps that my Fanakalo was rusty and they were referring to the language itself, sometimes called pidgin. Or perhaps it was a sophisticated joke at my expense, and they were feeding me a lot of pigeon shit.

Like many mysteries, the theft of the larger diamonds was solved in an arcane manner. I had, of course, reverted to type and would spend the evening in the local pub. I made a few drinking buddies, as you do, and started to learn how the mine worked with the local community. One night at the bar a local farmer mentioned he found it really weird that a pigeon had become tangled in tape. Alarm bells started to go off in my head. We discussed it a bit and, without showing too much excitement, I asked if he would bring me an example next time he saw it. The very next night he dropped in and parked himself on his barstool, a little later than usual. He pulled a thin-looking pigeon out of the rucksack he was carrying. There, taped to one leg, I discovered a three-carat stone. Amazing, diamond-carrying pigeons – who would have thought it?

At the security gates with their heavy-duty turnstiles, employees were checked very thoroughly on leaving the mine. But entering the mine was a much more relaxed affair. The thieves were taking in carrier pigeons concealed in their lunchboxes. On finding a modest-sized stone on the grease tables (the diamond extraction process uses the characteristic of diamonds to stick to grease in its concentration of the stones), it was taped to the leg of the pigeon, which was then released. The pigeon would fly up to the roof, which had open vents, and then presumably home. The farmer had been late because he had waited around with a shotgun where he had found the original pigeon and had shot one flying overhead.

I called senior management to a closed meeting the following day and, without the aid of a translator, gave them a full synopsis in fluent Fanakalo. Jaws dropped. They couldn't have been more surprised if I told them that every third man doesn't wash his hands after going to the bathroom and therefore, every third time they shake hands with a man, they are in effect holding his penis. Kissing... let's not go there. We planned an operation where we would check lunchboxes one by one as the employees came in for dayshift, carefully pulling them to one side once they were inside security and out-of-sight of the incoming workers, and immediately arresting anyone who apparently planned pigeon for lunch. There were no mobile phones in those days so those caught were unable to warn anyone else following behind. We interviewed them all, also obtaining enough evidence to implicate the translator. They were all fired, security on the tables was improved and netting installed on all of the open vents. Theft dropped somewhat, for a while.

I try not to make the mistake of underestimating anyone, and you have got to admire the local people in South Africa; they come up with amazingly clever and inventive ways of dealing with problems as they arise.

One story I heard in a bar was of a bus sent to transport patients from an asylum in Johannesburg to an asylum in Durban, a distance of nearly six hundred kilometres. The driver was doing well on the trip and, about halfway, decided to stop for a smoke break and to relieve himself. He wandered off the bus to do his stuff but failed to lock the door. On returning he discovered that his forty-five moonstruck inmates had disappeared into the bush. Now, you and I might have tried to herd the cats back into the bag, but the bus driver had a more ingenious solution. He just headed on to Durban with an empty bus. When he arrived at a stop close to the asylum, he loaded forty-five people on board and then drove them in, telling the guards at the gate that they would get angry and claim to be 'normal' and from the local area, but to ignore them and lock them up. You can just imagine them all claiming not to be mad, a clear indication of their insanity. Maybe we could try a similar project with City bankers? Just a thought.

Chapter 20 – Dog Diamonds

"Whoever thinks diamonds are a girl's best friend never had a dog." – Unknown

I did another diamond-related job for the Dog Group in Lesotho, a country completely surrounded by South Africa. This story illustrates just to what degree an assumption can be the mother of all stuff-ups. The Dog Group had attained the rights of a large diamond pipe called Lickaball. It was a huge diamondiferous kimberlite pipe that had been worked by artisanal miners for fifty or more years. They were working the weathered material on surface using shovels, sieves and wheelbarrows; hard graft wherever you do it. At quite some height above sea level, it also got nippy at night. The Dog Group reviewed the site, with its piles of spoil everywhere, and calculated that, over the fifty years, roughly one million six hundred thousand tonnes of material had been sifted through. We anticipated that quite a few stones would have been lost using the rudimentary processes of the artisanal miners and so, using the records of the government diamond buyers, we calculated around thirty-six carats per hundred tonnes as a likely average grade.

The deal agreed with the artisanal workers was that we would bring in a large Caterpillar digger and dozer to create a series of large trenches across the proposed pit, and a diamond Sortex machine for capturing the stones. There were eighty-nine workers when we did the deal, and each would receive the equivalent of twenty years of earnings. The real kicker for them was that we would allow them to keep working during the detailed exploration phase and, if we walked away, they could keep the equipment.

I was on the mountain when the first Cat came trundling over the horizon, as the sun was sinking to the horizon. The artisanal miners looked up from their labours and a resounding deep ululation spread across the site. Their delight was visible, tears of joy on their faces as they sang and danced late into the night. It was a most impressive and amazing spectacle, one that will remain with me all of my life.

The mother of all stuff-ups was in the calculation. Our assumption on the amount of material moved, plus the expected losses, was out by a factor of two. Once we started the large-scale bulk sampling, it rapidly became apparent that the grade was closer to twenty carats per hundred tonnes. Given we had built a business model predicate on thirty-six, it was difficult, to say the least, to dial back the assumptions we had made in order to create a business case that would get the investors excited to put more money in. This was clearly a Dog Project, and nobody would touch it. You should after all, always let sleeping dogs lie...

Today, I am happy to report that the mine is operational, that five hundred and fifty people are directly employed, and that it has a long-term, viable future. The final mother of all assumptions was to fail to realise that a single or series of big stones attracts considerably more per carat than your run-of-the-mill engagement ring; therefore, Lickaball, which keeps turning up an occasional giant, relies on the big dogs it occasionally finds... So, a lesson to all engineers and mine planners out there – always check your assumptions, then double-check them, and remember, every Dog has its day, and size is important.

Dog Corporation also had an exploration company in Kazakhstan. It wasn't too long before I was sent on a mission to look at one of their projects in the north of the country near Kustanai. I flew into Almaty and met up with the in-country manager, Bill Bosher. Bill was a no-nonsense Northerner who liked a few sherbets. We had a long lunch round the BBQ slurping down ice-cold beers and talking a whole load of bollocks. Bill had once been GM of Ashanti, and at one stage, when some consultants bitched and moaned too much, he escorted them to the front gate of the mine with their luggage and dumped them there with no transport. He didn't take prisoners and it was a 150km hike to the airport.

When it was time to visit the site, Bill did drive me back to the airport, where I boarded an Antonov AN-24, a Russian-made twin turboprop aircraft with rudimentary seating for forty-four people. After a few trips in Antonov's, we would fondly refer to them as washing machines, because that's what you feel like you've been through. The locals liked to transport their bleating goats and squawking chickens in them, and the din of the propellers meant it wasn't the most comfortable place to be. As I was lining up to board, I asked Bill how I would know the guy who was picking me up.

"Don't worry," he said with a twinkle in his eye, "you will definitely know Boris when you see him."

Of course, I did worry, added to which the dry horrors from the lunchtime alcohol started to make me hanker for water, any water. The mineral water on the flight tasted like flat coke. This, along with the cacophony and my exhaustion, made it a tedious four-hour flight. I was thankful when we arrived in Kustanai and the noise diminishing as the pilot killed the motors and the props span down to a standstill. I was parched – my mouth really did feel like the dry detritus at the bottom of a dirty parrot's cage. I gazed out of the window at the crowd of greeters standing by the exit gate. In Kustanai, the passengers picked up their own luggage which is dumped without ceremony on the tarmac by the flight crew. I gathered mine and ambled across to a metal gate in the fence protecting the runway. I spotted an enormous bear of a man waving two large bottles of vodka above his head, hopping around like a human dancing bear. Oh shit, I thought, that has to be Boris, and indeed it was.

Boris told me that Bill had called him and let him know that the vodka-drinking champion from England was coming to Kustanai to drink with him, and that he was looking forward to the challenge. It was a bloody long week. The water in Kustanai is highly saline. I used the old trick of drinking beer chasers. Once a bottle of beer is half drunk you can supposedly swig your shot but retain it in your mouth, then chase it immediately with a slug of beer. As you put the bottle of beer to your lips, you actually spit the vodka into the beer rather than drink it. Frequent visits to the toilet allow you to empty the contents on a regular basis. It was only in this way that I actually managed to survive. Boris was fun, but he loved to drink until he fell down. Every single night.

Dog also owned a copper porphyry project in Kazakhstan which was pretty low grade and started three hundred metres below ground. Any sensible person in the mining industry would dump this asset, knowing it was highly unlikely to ever be mined. Boss Dog thought differently of course; given his silky tongue and ability to put lipstick on a pig without it squealing too much, he needed me to dress it up in the Information Memorandum I was preparing on the project. I sent him the business case model and it came back with "Make this give a better return" scrawled on the front. Hard as I tried, the costs of extraction made the project, at best, marginal. Boss Dog was not happy.

"What can we do to make this more economic?" he growled.

"Well, other than detonate a massive atomic bomb on top of it, and remove three hundred metres of ground, there is nothing you can do."

What was somewhat concerning about my bomb suggestion was that he really did seem to think about it for around twenty seconds. I was starting to worry that the corporate world was stuffed with madmen. When an opportunity arose to leave the thriving metropolis of London for the edge of the world in far eastern Russia and join the big boys' club by becoming a director, I grabbed it with both hands; I joined a silver-mining company which was in the process of funding and developing a brownfield mine in Magadan.

Era 3

The Big Boys' Club...

"The challenge of leadership is to be strong, but not rude; be kind, but not weak; be bold, but not a bully; be thoughtful, but not lazy; be humble, but not timid; be proud, but not arrogant; have humour, but without folly." – Jim Rohn

"It's difficult to be humorous about the serious business of leadership." – Jack Shaft

Chapter 21: The Ruletka Mine

"So cold I got hail when I turned on the shower." – Let's get wordy

I had taken the opportunity to become the Finance Director of the Ruletka Mine. My first role as a director involved preparing the accounts to both Russian and GAAP standards (Generally Accepted Accounting Principles), managing contracts and payments, and assisting in the raising of funds for the rebuild project. Whenever I mentioned where I was working to Russians, they took in a sharp breath, before politely changing the subject. Other nationalities didn't have a clue where Magadan was.

Ruletka had been run by the Soviets as a pure silver mine up in the Kolyma region of Magadan, eastern Russia. The Kolyma was the most notorious region of the Soviet Union for labour camps. In Stalin's time, political and criminal prisoners were shipped across the country to Vladivostok, loaded into the holds of ships, and transported by sea to the port town of Magadan on the Sea of Okhotsk. The sea around Magadan freezes in winter to a thickness of more than a metre. Local residents drive onto the frozen sea and cut holes in the ice through which to fish. The temperatures in Magadan hover around minus forty Celsius during the winter, with an average temperature of minus seven Celsius for the year. It's a little nippy.

If the prisoners started getting restless, the sailors would spray them with icy water, in some cases freezing their human cargo to death. Once unloaded in the port, they were taken to the gulags, used as forced labour to build a road into the Kolyma to allow access to the vast golden riches hidden within. Six million prisoners took this one-way journey, but only three hundred and fifty thousand people now remain in the territory. The maths is relatively easy, but the story is incredibly grim. It is here where many of the horrors of the Stalinist USSR were perpetrated and it is this bleak place that Aleksandr Solzhenitsyn wrote about in The Gulag Archipelago, as this quote outlines;

If it were possible for any nation to fathom another people's bitter experience through a book, how much easier its future fate would become and how many calamities and mistakes it could avoid. But it is very difficult. There always is this fallacious belief: It would not be the same here; here such things are impossible. Alas, all the evil of the twentieth century is possible everywhere on Earth.

However, for all Solzhenitsyn's beautiful prose, I find Varlam Shalamov a more poetic and compelling writer about the Kolyma:

Cold, hunger and sleeplessness rendered any friendship impossible, and Dugaev – despite his youth – understood the falseness of the belief that friendship could be tempered by misery and tragedy. For friendship to be friendship, its foundation had to be laid before living conditions reached that last border beyond which no human emotion was left to a man – only mistrust, rage and lies. Dugaev remembered well the northern proverb that listed the three commandments of prison life: Don't believe, don't fear, don't ask. If bones could freeze, then the brain could also be dulled, and the soul could freeze over. And the soul shuddered and froze, perhaps to remain frozen forever.

It is my hope that those quotes give you a brief sense of the terrifying history of the place as well as of the ever-penetrating cold. There is a song about Magadan which goes... "Twelve months of winter, and all the rest of the year is summer."

It was from the ebullient city of London that I arrived in this godforsaken corner of the world. Magadan was an eight hour direct flight from Moscow on a plane on which one would do best to avoid the toilet. It has always been difficult for me to imagine any of the countless beautiful Russian women I have met actually frequenting one of these facilities. The floor is usually covered by an inch of what I can only describe as 'pustulent ooze', with an ammoniacal smell that could stop a charging rhino dead in its tracks at fifty metres. If you need to use the toilet, it is recommended that in advance you develop strong thigh and calf muscles so you can hover safely well clear of the rim. If by chance you were to touch it, the chances are you would become stuck like a fly in a Venus flytrap, and then be gradually consumed by the rancid ooze.

That Magadan was cold should by now be clear, but the locals dressed for it. As one of my charming lady friends remarked when I commented on her beautiful mink coat, and how she would probably have paint thrown all over it in London:

"In Magadan, it takes forty dumb animals to make one of these coats, and one helluva dumb one not to wear it."

One of my first meetings after arrival was with our local partner. He was a short balding fella with a deep growl of a voice. He took me to one side after the meeting and intoned seriously, "Jack, it's cold here." Patting his left hip, he added, "You need one devoushka [lady] here, and" – patting the right hip – "one devoushka here." I laughed, though I think he was deadly serious.

The Ruletka team quickly set about arranging the funds for the recommissioning of the mine. We prepared the project so as to present it in the best light and had a cluster of IFC bankers come in to do due diligence on the assets and the in-country team. They stayed for three days, during which time we showed them the old underground areas and plant and all of the available infrastructure, roads, power lines and capacity, plus the other amenities in the locality. We had a pleasant meal with our partner and the Governor of the province, Valentine Svetkov, a huge man with hands the size of large shovels. It was all going swimmingly, and all the signs were positive. In the final hours of the visit, we had a wrap-up meeting between the senior team and the IFC bankers. Again, all was going well, when the head of the IFC delegation turned to the translator, who was in the room to assist with communication with the senior Russians on the team, and asked the seemingly innocent question:

"So, what's it like working with Jack then?"

She thought for a second and answered, "I love working with Jack, he is such a creative accountant." There was a stunned silence. The westerners in the group were appalled.

We managed to rescue the situation, explaining it was lost in translation, but it took a mighty effort of persuasion given that it is not an unreasonable to be concerned if your finance director is a bit on the 'creative' side. Especially in the light of the Bre-X.

In the end, we received the funding we needed - about forty million dollars in equity from the shareholders, and another sixty million dollars from IFC in a syndicated loan. It was great to be employing people and making real things happen.

The only way to bring in all of the heavy equipment was along the "road of bones", so called on account of all the prisoners that had died during its construction in Stalin's time. These ice roads were smoothed out with powerful graders as soon as winter set in, which enabled traffic into the hinterland. Shalamov, in his Kolyma tales, gives a moving description of how prisoners would physically move the snow with their bodies to clear the road.

Trampling the snow

"How do you trample a road through virgin snow? One man walks ahead, sweating and cursing, barely able to put one foot in front of the other, getting stuck every minute in the deep, porous snow. This man goes a long way ahead, leaving a trail of uneven black holes. He gets tired, lies down in the snow, lights a cigarette, and the tobacco smoke forms a blue cloud over the brilliant white snow. Even when he has moved on, the smoke cloud still hovers over his resting place. The air is almost motionless. Roads are always made on calm days, so that human labour is not swept away by wind. A man makes his own landmarks in this unbounded snowy waste: a rock, a tall tree. He steers his body through the snow like a helmsman steering a boat along a river, from one bend to the next.

The narrow, uncertain footprints he leaves are followed by five or six men walking shoulder to shoulder. They step around the footprints, not in them. When they reach a point agreed on in advance, they turn around and walk back so as to trample down this virgin snow where no human foot has trodden. And thus, a trail is blazed. People, convoys of sleds, tractors can use it. If they had walked in single file, there would have been a barely passable narrow trail, a path, not a road: a series of holes that would be harder to walk over than virgin snow. The first man has the hardest job, and when he is completely exhausted, another man from this pioneer group of five steps forward. Of all the men following the trailblazer, even the smallest, the weakest must not just follow someone else's footprints but must walk a stretch of virgin snow himself. As for riding tractors or horses, that is the privilege of the bosses, not the underlings."

It was a long way from London and the last night of the proms.

Chapter 22: Nuts

"Every cloud has a silver lining, but sometimes it's a little difficult to get it to the mint." Don Marquis

In Magadan's short summer, the snow melts and the ground un-freezes to the permafrost. The rivers become raging torrents and much of the road becomes an impassable quagmire. The only way in or out of the hinterland is by helicopter.

On one of the helicopter flights up to the mine site the cloud cover was pretty low. The pilot was creeping up a valley, under the clouds, above a fairly sizeable river. Leon Kania, our logistics guy and an ex-marine from the US, started to tremble beside me. What I know about helicopters and their flight patterns can be written on the inside of a ping-pong ball in letters six feet high. Until this moment I had been sitting lost in thought, dreaming of beaches, piña coladas and being smothered in chocolate which was being licked off by scantily clad damsels. My mind cleared instantly – something was less than perfect in Leon Kania's world. The 'copter itself continued to vibrate like a washing machine on speed and the rocky outcrops seemed remarkably close to the rotor blades. The 'copter suddenly dropped downwards, causing Leon to shit himself, as we bumped hard onto what appeared to be a small island in the middle of the river. The pilot, cursing vociferously in Russian, opened the door and climbed nimbly onto the top of the machine, brandishing what looked like an enormous spanner and a lump hammer. We vacated the helicopter quickly through the same door. Images of being consumed by a raging inferno caused by aviation fuel rushed through my mind – this wasn't how it was supposed to end for me. Where was the foaming pint of IPA? Where was the steaming hot Cornish pasty? Where was my leopard skin stretched limousine? The pilot proceeded to apply the spanner to a massive nut on top of the rotors, belting it like a blacksmith in a speed hammering contest.

"What's he doing?" I asked Leon.

"He's tightening the Jesus nut," he replied quietly as he started to clean himself up with some handy toilet paper.

"The Jesus nut... Why is it called that?"

"Because if it comes off, the blades go walkabout, and the chopper falls out of the sky. The next time you speak, it will be to talk to Jesus."

I got the picture. The Jesus nut, or Jesus pin, is a slang term for the retaining nut that holds the main rotor to the helicopter mast. Leon cleaned himself up in the freezing waters and we waited a couple of hours for the clouds to clear. While awaiting rescue, we and our Russian buddies swigged down a handy couple of litres of vodka not allowed on site. If we were going to die, we might as well be happily numb when it happened... The chopper pilot certainly seemed to think so as he toasted being alive.

The mine rebuild was proceeding well, though I had my doubts about some of the costings, which looked a bit expensive. The Russian managers assured me that it was hugely expensive to do anything in Magadan and, reluctantly, I accepted their point. I did however force them to obtain three quotes on every large project or item of equipment over twenty-five grand: I noticed they then split up projects into chunks smaller than this threshold. They also seemed to outsource purchases to one particular standalone company, which then bought the items for them. It all felt pretty fishy. The GM was a Canadian guy who walked like a duck. He wasn't the first choice, but it isn't easy to bring quality people to Magadan, they had engaged me after all.

A global financial crisis hit in 1998 and several Russian banks went bust, including the one where we had our money for the mine build. Fortunately, I had only been moving cash in from Canada in small tranches. Just enough to cover the next couple of weeks so only half a million dollars became semi-frozen. While we couldn't take much out, we could use it to pay taxes to the state, and I developed a cute system for slowly extracting more using all of my limited charms.

Nearly all chief accountants in Russia are women, as was the bank manager. My modus operandi was to buy a box of chocolates and a bottle of champagne for my weekly visit to the bank. My translator would sail past the waiting accountants and into her office, announcing that her foreign gentleman was here to visit. I would breeze in, graciously offer her the chocs and the fizz, and compliment her on her charming earrings, or anything else remotely worthy of admiration. Her favourite earrings were two elephants, with what looked like noodles on their ears. She would coquettishly serve me tea and biscuits, fluttering outlandish stick-on eyelashes, while I flirted back outrageously.

"Let us speak only in Russian," she purred, in the hope that I would dismiss the translator. My Russian wasn't nearly good enough and besides, being attacked by a Russian cougar surrounded by jangling elephants was not an experience I wanted to regret someday.

I was the youngest of twenty-three foreigners in the city port of Magadan, which had a total population of around a hundred and fifty thousand. Having the young English gentleman fawn over her gave the bank manager bragging rights; every week she would release another ten-thousand-dollar chunk of our money, which enabled me to pay office bills and salaries.

However, the downside of this charade was that we didn't have nearly enough cash to continue the construction work. The board of directors was reluctant to use another Russian bank given the ongoing crisis so we set up a process whereby I would fly to Vancouver, pick up a serious wedge of cash in one hundred dollar bills, and then fly back into Russia with it in a money belt. This wad weighed between three and five kilograms and was worth up to five hundred thousand dollars. I swore my Chief Accountant to secrecy. People got whacked in Russia for far smaller sums, and I didn't want to become a part of those statistics.

Chapter 23: Invaluable Dumps

'Legged over' means to be duped or seen coming. Not to be confused with getting your leg over. – Jack Shaft

At one point in my cash mule phase, I had to fly in the long way around because the carrier into Magadan from Anchorage had stopped flying. Usually I would fly the route Vancouver – Seattle – Anchorage – Magadan. Now I had to travel the long way round; Vancouver – London – Moscow – Magadan. A tedious journey at the best of times; even if everything went to plan it would take around twenty-six hours. The vindaloo curry with beer chasers the night of departure from Vancouver was probably not the most intelligent move I have ever made. As I staggered into the BA flight toilet for the third time on the leg from Vancouver to London, wobbling my money belt through the narrow door, I realised that this wasn't your standard-grade food poisoning 'shit it all out in one load' event. I may have contracted amoeboid dysentery, and there were a long set of flights ahead. I considered bailing in London for a couple of days, but the reckless folly of a desire to get the job done drove me on, that and the anticipation that I would never see my luggage again.

I boarded and then had my final shit on the London to Moscow leg, in the hopes of avoiding a trip to the Russian cesspit on the Magadan flight. I had a transfer at Moscow's Domodedovo airport. Clutching my stomach, both to protect the money belt as well as to try and staunch the ominous rumblings, I boarded the next flight. The de-icer sprayed the wings and I closed my eyes, hoping for the sweet release of sleep. My knowledge of Russian was just about good enough to understand the pilot's announcement over the intercom – there would be a delay. Shit! Shit! Shit! Shit! Shit!

I turned to a fragrant group of Russian fishermen and asked them if they spoke English. They didn't of course, but my terrible Russian made them all laugh uproariously. They thrust a big mug of vodka in my face and ordered me to drink and, as you know, an Englishman can't say no.

Now before you accuse me of flagrant idiocy (again), you need to understand that the relationship between a Russian and a bottle of vodka is a mystical, even spiritual, one. Indeed, it is the anaesthetic used to endure the eternal operation that is their life. At this point, I should probably re-tell their anecdote about vodka drinking in Russia that will give an insight into why I ended up drinking with a bunch of Russian fishermen for six hours before passing out.

The fishermen believe that you should start every day with a spoonful of honey. You should let this settle for a minute and then chase it with strong black coffee. Immediately after that, you drink a shot of vodka. The thinking goes a bit like this: when the honey arrives in the stomach, all the bugs jump on it to get a feed. You then blind them with thick, black coffee and in the confusion you kill them off with the vodka. Their clinching argument was that milk gives you strength. But drink three glasses of milk and try moving a wall. You can't. Drink three shots of vodka and the wall moves by itself.

The plane remained on the tarmac in Moscow for eight hours by which time it had been some thirty hours since I had left my Vancouver hotel room. Fortunately, by this time, I was also comatose. I awoke about half-way to Magadan and saw out of the corner of my eye that the fishermen were still at it – talking even more bollocks than before, if that were possible. They were trading 'Biggest crab I ever caught' stories, and trust me, they had crabs. I tried to maintain a position of repose despite the gurgling and rumblings going on down below. Just another four hours then plus a forty-minute car ride to go until the sanctuary of the beautifully pristine toilet in my flat. Bliss was on the horizon – I knew I could make it. I kept my eyes shut tight and tried to think of anything to take my mind off the slowly passing time. How important does a person have to be before they are considered assassinated instead of just murdered? You know that little indestructible black box that is used on planes, why can't they make the whole plane with the same substance? Why is it called taking a dump when you're actually leaving it? Ouch. Wrong question again. Thirty-six hours down and counting.

I managed to maintain this mummy like pose until the plane landed. I was desperate for a shit – absolutely bursting. Cramps were coming in waves, but I was sure I could make it. The pilot came on the intercom. I heard the word 'Irkutsk', and looked out of the window. Horror show... It wasn't Magadan. The flight had been diverted due to bad weather. The plane would refuel, and we would resume our journey in four hours. Forty hours journey so far.

I wondered if I could make it after all. They let us off the plane into the terminal building and I staggered around in search of the toilet. I found it by following the smell and tried to enter. The toilet had probably not been cleaned since Stalin's time. It was appalling. I could see festering turds on the floor through the open doorway. No way could I use that, not even holding my nose.

Hiding from the fishermen, I sat huddled on a bare metal seat as far as possible from the waste repository threatening to gas the passengers and airport workers. I swear I could see a toxic cloud around the latrines, and that even flies were expiring mid-flight. Once again, I nodded off into blissful oblivion, dreaming of gleaming white porcelain, the smell of bleach and the joy of empty, pain-free bowels. At last, the skies began to clear, and they called us to board the flight. I staggered on, the image of my pristine bathroom still etched into my imagination. Forty-five hours now since I had set off; a four-and-a-half hour flight plus the ride into town lay between me and my flat.

The spasms were coming in waves now, and the smell from the aircraft toilets, while still foul, didn't seem quite as obnoxious as it had before. It seemed you could get used to it.

I tried breathing just like I had been taught to support my wife through her labour pains. It helped a little. Then we hit turbulence. Not the mild, rock-you- about-in-your-seat-a-bit turbulence. No, this was eye of the storm stuff with people-screaming-and-drinks-flying-everywhere turbulence. It lasted around thirty minutes during which time passengers were unhappily sharing the contents of their glasses with their neighbours, and their neighbours' neighbours. The plane began to shake and fall. The heads of passengers who were not seat-belted were slamming the ceiling.

I clenched my jaw and buttocks and gripped the armrests. If I was going to die here, I was going to do it with all of my shit inside me, I told myself. Just as I thought it would never end, we came out of the storm. Another half-hour passed, and the plane started to descend. The pilot came in at a low trajectory, hitting the runway at high speed, as is the Russian way, and jammed on the reverse thrust. We skidded to a halt and taxied to the terminal. Fifty hours so far...

I limped off the flight in the direction of the terminal. I reached the building and was greeted the by the now very familiar Russian latrine smell and... coffee. The almost sweet smell of coffee. That fruity, lightly caramelised almost nutty almost smoky beautiful smell that was always a sure thing to make me crap, and it didn't disappoint. I ran to the disgusting, shit-encrusted bog, which was void of people. Only a madman would go into one of these and even then, only under immense duress. I dropped my trousers and kecks and let flow an immense stream of putrefied shit. The relief was instantaneous and immeasurable; it was the most pleasurable shit I had ever taken – better than any aspirin. Just as well I didn't make it to my flat because I would have blocked the sewers for the whole building.

The mine reconstruction process continued. Despite the financial crisis in Russia, we managed to cajole cash out of the banks for bankruptcy protection and we continued carrying in cash and buying major capital items from outside Russia. However, my suspicions about the practices of some of the other members of the leadership team kept on growing and it was clear that they were wise that I was on to them and some of the corrupt practices that were occurring. I soon got wind that this same team had pulled similar stunts in another part of the Former Soviet Union. Further, it was likely that the government would be stimulated to force a re-tender of the mining licence, even though the company rightly owned the assets on the ground, having acquired them from the liquidator. The final pin in the balloon occurred when a tender for the civil works on a new tailings dam came in at three times the quote I had received from another company. When I confronted them, instead of backing down, they insisted that the latter company was not a company qualified for the work. Pure bullshit, of course, and the idealistic me sent the details of this to the chairman along with a prediction that the perpetrators would engineer a re-tender of the licence which the company would lose. The chairman immediately sent his CEO, Josh, to site to carry out an investigation. Josh interviewed everyone (including me) over the course of three days. I sincerely believed that they would fire the guilty parties and we could then reset.

Josh came to me at the end of his visit.

"Jack, I am ninety percent sure you are right in everything you have said. However, there were five people named on the IFC loan document and you were only one of them. If we fire the others, we will have to go back to IFC and build a whole new team which will take months. However, if we let you go, this is easily explained. (You being such a creative accountant I read in the subtext). We will pay you the six months' separation payment, but I am afraid you are going to have to go."

I was devastated. I really expected that "real" companies would look to act morally rather than only expeditiously. Tell the truth, and the truth will set you free; it did in this case for I was freed onto the next plane out.

In the end, the dirty tricks played out as I had anticipated – the licence was re-tendered, and the company lost the bid. The forty million dollars of equity that had been sunk into assets on the ground in Magadan became mired in legal spaghetti, and the company and its shareholders effectively lost everything they had in Russia. Did it help being proved right? Not really – by that stage I had lost my job, had a dint in my reputation, and I had moved on. I had learned a valuable lesson however, when it comes to money, ethics and morals are fungible.

Chapter 24: Wherever?

"If you don't know where you are going, any road will get you there." – Lewis Carroll

At least I had some money in the bank. However, the separation pay out from the company would attract significant tax if I returned to the UK and it would be better for me to delay my return home into the following tax year. I headed for Cyprus to stay with my parents and write the book I knew was brewing inside me. I decided to stop off in Kiev for a couple of weeks to see my old buddy Smallbone who was working on a project there. It would be many years before I finally reached Cyprus, and this book has been bubbling away for twenty more years, but here it is at long last.

I arrived in Kiev during a breath-taking autumn of red and gold in the parks, and temperatures of twenty to twenty-five degrees Celsius. I walked and walked the streets. Kiev has wonderful monuments, churches and monasteries to visit; my personal favourite site is the Museum of Unnecessary Things, a delightful repository of discarded, useless objects, where once fashionable engineering trash is given a second chance, where you can view any manner of first-world junk. Even better, it's free of charge. It's amazing what the human mind will come up with once unfettered from the daily need to hunt and roast a corpse or gather a pile of nuts and seeds to stave off imminent starvation. The museum displays hundreds of Lenin statue arms, dusty fax machines and rusting typewriters, and untold numbers of Benny Hill videotapes. According to the guidebook, over one million items have made their way to this unusual attraction since it opened in 1943.

If old Benny Hill videos and crusty superseded technology don't pique your interest, this peculiar locale also houses a number of at one time ground-breaking historical inventions, including the world's first vacuum cleaner, a feather duster and the prototype of a baby's pram. These items were all designed to free up more time for Soviet womanhood to join the fight for a socialist utopia. In what I can only imagine is a bit of Slavic humour, the museum is fittingly located on the grounds of the Kievgorvtorresursy recycling plant.

The museum is closed on Saturdays and Sundays when you might think that the hard-working socialist toiler would want some weekend relief from their industrial confinement. Despite this oversight concerning the mental health of the proletariat, the friendly security guard allowed me in to wander around and have a poke at the ingenious junk people have invented and discarded over the years. It was a great playground for an engineer nursing a bruised ego.

Smallbone had become something of a big swinging dick in the consultancy company where he worked. He lived in a flat just off Khreshchatyk, Kiev's main street. It felt safe, friendly and dynamic, this being the early years of the split from the Soviet Union though one needs to remember the dark past was still reverberating. Every now and then, the military would pile out of their barracks and have tank races up and down Khreshchatyk to remind everybody who was really in charge.

Smallbone's company was implementing a project on 'In-Company Change Programmes' aimed at assisting Ukraine to move from a socialist to a capitalist economy. Interventions in marketing, accounting, strategy and operations were undertaken by western experts, and the processes and methodologies were recorded. They had targeted twenty-three companies in various segments of the economy for their interventions, including mines, sausage factories and vodka manufacturers. Just as I arrived on the scene, the chief of party (essentially the project's MD) had been "recalled to Washington." The project had been given a cure notice by the funder, which meant that it had thirty days to come up with a new plan to achieve its objectives or funding would be withdrawn. Smallbone had just been made the new chief of party, but he wasn't celebrating. In desperation, he asked if I could look at writing the dissemination component of the new proposal. Clearly, if he'd had any other option he would have taken it, but Hobson here was in town and at a loose end, and mining, sausages and vodka were all in my sweet spot.

I set about writing a presentation about how to take the lessons learned from the In-Company Change

158

Programme and disseminate them to as many people as possible. Initially, we thought about equipping Ukrainian trainers to train ever larger groups of disciples, using case-study examples of how capitalist management techniques had been successfully implemented in real Ukrainian companies. The idea was to strip away the excuses that would always be heard from Ukrainian bosses – these approaches are all very well in America, but they wouldn't work here. We planned on presenting them to companies all over Ukraine in seminars and train-the-trainer workshops. When I presented the dissemination plan to the donor, what really grabbed their attention was the idea of recording video case studies and training programmes with voiceovers from the presenters on CD-ROMs. We could print tens of thousands of these and distribute them to universities, technical colleges, companies, councils and local consultancies. The donor loved the idea, and that, along with other changes made by the consultant specialists, convinced them to continue funding the project.

I felt I had done my piece and I was just in the process of booking my ticket out of Kiev having enjoyed a splendid autumn when Smallbone collared me.

"You're not going anywhere, mate. You sold the idea to the grown-ups, now you better bloody well deliver it. They want you to stay."

With that, I became the dissemination leader for the next twelve months, making videos, recording training programmes and making a CD-ROM with everything on it, in three languages: English, Ukrainian and Russian. Of course, in the process I had to prick around in the mines and eat a lot of sausage washed down with industrial alcohol. Home sweet home.

I discovered that one of the joys of working on this sort of assignment is having a ringside view of the local culture and building lasting friendships with local people. I loved it.

One very special part of Slavic culture is their love of anecdotes. In English, the word anecdote suggests a short, amusing or interesting story about a real incident or person. Starting in the early twentieth century however, its meaning in the Slavic world changed and anecdotes became fictional short (or often even long) stories told for the purpose of making a political point in a darkly cynical way while having a good laugh. This also marked the beginning of their universal popularity throughout the Soviet Union.

However, before I get into telling you my favourite anecdotes, I think it's important to understand the historical backdrop as this explains just how risky telling anecdotes could be under previous regimes.

Chapter 25: Slavic Society and Anecdotage

"Russia is a riddle wrapped in a mystery inside an enigma."
– Winston Churchill

At this point, it would be useful to take a look at the dark history of the seventy or so years of the failed communist experiment that was the USSR. During World War 1, the imperious but incompetent Tsar lost the loyalty of his military, and two competing regimes seized power: a liberal Provisional Government and a mildly socialist Soviet. It didn't take long for this new bunch of fresh-air wasters to lose street cred, thereby allowing a third political movement, the Bolsheviks, to seize the reins of authority. They were extreme socialists, who, under the leadership of Lenin, drove the bloody socialist revolution in October 1917 and its murderous dictatorship. To consolidate their power, they ushered in the 'Red Terror', using the somewhat twisted logic that in order to establish peaceful control, you first needed a bloodthirsty period of anarchy, murder and suppression. A new political police force, the Cheka, undertook summary executions of 'bourgeois hostages' on charges of 'counterrevolutionary provocation'. A sort of bloody 'drain the swamp' of the old bungling stupidocracy who would be replaced with a new idiocracy. That, of course, could never happen today with all of our reliable checks and balances. No, of course not.

Under Stalin's regime, the Soviet press ironically described him as 'Great', 'Beloved', 'Bold', 'Wise', 'Inspirer' and 'Genius'. With the Soviet populace as his 'children', he was a caring yet strong father figure, who simply had to cause a few million unnatural deaths all for the sake of a brighter future. The exact number of unnatural deaths due to Stalin over the course of his thirty-year murderous regime is subject to much debate; however, no-one disputes that it runs into the many millions.

Stalin ordered 'Dekulakisation' (1929 -1932), the liquidation of an entire class of people. This led to the deportations, starvation and deaths of between six hundred thousand and five million 'Kulaks' (richer, landowning peasants) as part of Stalin's five-year plan and goal of forced collectivisation. Having cemented his position in history as one of the bloodiest dictators to have ever lived, Stalin decided to double down with the Great Purges between 1936 and 1941. In this new terror ploy, he orchestrated a further 1.2 million deaths through state repression, relocation and deportation of any perceived political opponents and ethnic minority groups. This included the creation of the Gulags. Between 1934 and 1953 around 18 million people were sent to these state-run forced-labour prison camps across the USSR. Six million or so were sent to the Magadan summer camp. Over one million died in detention through execution, starvation and disease, and many more were released to a certain death from the cold.

However, why have your perceived political opponents die a useless death in the camps, when they could provide benefit as German lead collectors in the front lines? In Command No. 227 of 1942, Stalin ordered the creation of penal battalions for each front; half a million Soviet soldiers from 1942-45 were either court-martialled or disciplined for flimsy reasons and sent to these penal battalions. The under-equipped, under-supplied units were prevented from retreating from the most dangerous frontlines by being shot by so-called blocking detachments stationed behind them.

When Stalin died in March 1953, Nikita Khrushchev became leader of the Party. In February 1956, he ushered in a period of 'de-Stalinisation', shocking the world by making a secret speech denouncing Stalin to the 20th Party Congress. Khrushchev attempted to improve Soviet living standards and allow greater freedom in cultural and intellectual life. Outside of the USSR, Khrushchev's period in office was marked by a series of crises; the shooting down of an American U2 spy plane over the Soviet Union in 1960, the building of the Berlin Wall in 1961 and, most significantly, the Cuban Missile Crisis in 1962, which brought the world to the brink of nuclear war. Internally, the USSR continued its suppression of its satellite states in Eastern Europe and, in 1956, an uprising in Hungary against Communist rule was brutally suppressed. By 1964, Khrushchev had alienated much of the Soviet elite and was forced to retire by his opponents, led by Leonid Brezhnev.

Brezhnev consolidated his inept rule by overseeing a wondrous new period of economic stagnation and widespread corruption, undermining public faith in any superiority of the Soviet model, with shortages of just about everything. At least he wasn't murdering everybody he disagreed with, and shortages meant hunger, but not starvation. So that was a small leap forward.

1985-91 saw the rise to power of Mikhail Gorbachev, heralding serious efforts to reform the moribund economy (perestroika), free up political debate (glasnost), and bring an end to the crippling cost of the continuing Cold War. Gorbachev gradually lost control of the reform processes, probably due to his attempt to rein in the alcoholism of the local population in a failed attempt at prohibition. Without bloody suppression, he also lost control of the country's satellite states, leading ultimately to the collapse of Communist rule in Eastern Europe and the eventual implosion of the Soviet Union itself.

So, it is against this history that the Russian people tell their anecdotes. Even though there were times when telling of such stories was a capital offence, they became a popular form of creativity and a much cherished pastime. Anecdotes in Russia represent folk literature and there are many traditions associated with them. When you're telling an anecdote, it doesn't matter if it's been heard before. Telling a 'borodatiy' (bearded and therefore very old) anecdote in a compelling way is very much appreciated.

Here are a few of my favourites, learned from locals over many a shot of vodka.

Evil dictators

An old priest died and went to Heaven. He was asked if he had one last wish before entering. He replied that he would like to have a guided tour of Hell. They began in one of the deepest pits, reserved for those whose lives had been comprised of utter evil. In the middle he saw a lake of boiling shit, in which were standing Hitler and Stalin. Stalin was up to his waist in it and Hitler up to his nose.

"That's outrageous," said the priest. "Why should Hitler be punished more than Stalin? I suffered under both, and Stalin was just as evil as Hitler."

"You don't understand," said his guide. "Stalin is standing on the shoulders of Lenin."

It is quite normal, a few sentences into your recitation, to inquire whether your audience has heard this specific anecdote before. They will reply with, "Come on! Tell us!" This, in Russian, is code for, "Yes, of course, we have heard this anecdote before, but we want to hear YOU tell it."

Torture

A mummy was found in Egypt. The archaeologists could not determine its origin but a Soviet advisor offered his help. The mummy was delivered to the Soviet embassy and two hours later, the Soviet advisor appeared and said, "His name was Amun the 23rd."

"How did you find out?"

"He confessed," the advisor said.

Bravery

A Russian, a Frenchman and an American argued as to whose people was the bravest.

The American said, "We take ten cars, one of which has no brakes. We throw the dice, each of us gets in a car, and we drive fast on mountain roads. Afterwards one of us ends up in hospital, and the other nine visit him there."

"That's nothing," the Frenchman said. "We take ten girls, one of them has syphilis. We throw the dice, each one of us gets a girl, and we make love to them all the night. Afterwards one of us ends up in hospital, and the other nine visit him."

The Russian said, "Childs play. Ten of us gather in an apartment for a party, even though we know that one among us must be an informer. We tell political jokes all night, and then the next day nine of us are in jail, and the informer visits us."

Shortages

Stalin is dead and things have begun to lighten up a bit, relatively speaking. An old couple live in an apartment in Moscow and the woman sends her husband to buy some meat for supper.

After queuing for the obligatory three hours, he gets to the counter and the woman says, "No more meat, meat finished."

He cracks and starts raving, "I fought in the Revolution, I fought for Lenin in the First World War and for Stalin in the Second World War and we are still in this shit?"

A KGB agent walks up to him and tells him to calm down, adding, "Don't forget what happened to people like you back in the old days," making a gun shape with his hand. The old man goes back to his apartment, empty-handed.

His wife says, "They're out of meat?"

He replies, "It's worse than you think, they're out of bullets."

Living in Paradise

An Englishman, a Frenchman and a Russian are all in the Hermitage looking at a beautiful painting of Adam and Eve in the Garden of Eden. The Englishman rocks back on his heels, clears his throat and quivers his stiff upper lip.

"Sorry, old chaps" – for being British he has to apologise for everything – "look at the beautiful landscape, the warm sunlit uplands, the verdant green pastures, the charming babbling brook. See Adam, giving his only apple to the lady like a proper gentleman. This painting is set in England."

"*Mais non*," said the Frenchman, pursing his lips and giving a Gallic shrug of the shoulders. "Look at the beautiful sexy couple 'oo 'ave just made lurve. Look at their voluptuous naked bodies, and the sensual way in which Adam is offering the rosy fruit to his lovely Eve. Zis 'as to be a picture of France."

"Nyet," says the Russian forthrightly. "Look at them. They have no clothes, they have no home. They only have one apple to eat, and they are told they are living in paradise. This is Russia."

Shortly after joining the team in Kiev, I needed to find my own place to get out of Smallbone's hair. I started flat-hunting, and flippantly put 'comedian' as my occupation on the agency's application form. Unlike everywhere else, though, being a funny man doesn't quite cut the mustard in Russia. On my first viewing of a potential flat, the landlord asked me, "Comedian, is that a serious profession?"

I responded, "Yeah, well, the last time I worked, nobody laughed." He didn't get it, and neither did I.

Chapter 26: Bedding in

"I am foreign, so I must be depraved and rich." – Jack Shaft

My new role in the Ukrainian project proved a good deal of fun. I enjoyed making films about the implementation of market economy reforms in these lumbering behemoth enterprises. However, it was clear that, as soon as the western "experts" withdrew, most of these new approaches would be abandoned, with a reversion to the government-controlled command economy way of doing things. The key to real change, in my view, lay in the distribution of the CD-ROMs to younger, more flexible minds. We started with the creation of an interactive CD-ROM with all the training materials and films included in three languages. This was effectively a mini MBA course with real-life illustrative in-country case studies.

The software was developed in Kharkiv, a ten hour train ride away, by a dynamic new local company. Kharkiv had been a code-hacking centre in the Soviet era and was stuffed full of brilliant software engineers. They did a fabulous job of creating the product but dealing with change requests and transporting it back and forth between Kharkiv and Kiev for testing was proving to be time-consuming. It was better to take the test team to Kharkiv and do real-time changes on the live product on their systems. I set off on the overnight train with a team of four ladies who were working on the project. When we arrived in

Kharkiv early the next morning, I took them to the city's Central Hotel. My idea was to rent a small room so we could take it in turns to shower and change. At the reception desk of the hotel, with my four damsels in tow, I asked for a single room with a shower. The hotel manager eyed the four ladies behind me appreciatively and then asked, "Would Sir like a bigger bed?"

Clearly much had changed since the austerity of Soviet times. Indeed, this brings to mind another favourite anecdote about how attractive communism had been for the average citizen:

Ivanov applied to join the Communist Party. The Party committee conducted an interview to test his suitability.

"Comrade Ivanov, do you smoke?"

"Yes, I do a little."

"Do you know that Comrade Lenin did not smoke and advised other Communists not to smoke?"

"If Comrade Lenin said so, I shall cease smoking."

"Do you drink?"

"Yes, I do occasionally."

"Comrade Lenin strongly condemned drunkenness."

"Then I shall cease drinking."

"Comrade Ivanov, what about loose women? Do you have amorous relationships with women other than your wife?"

"Once I..."

"Do you know that comrade Lenin strongly condemned amoral behaviour?"

"If Comrade Lenin condemned it, I shall never stray again."

"Comrade Ivanov, will you be ready to sacrifice your life for the Party?"

"Of course I am ready... Who needs such a life?"

The project proved to be a success in the eyes of the donor organisation, and one of my proudest moments was finding large numbers of the CD-ROMs being sold in the many black-market shops and stalls in Kiev. We gave away all of our printed copies for free, so these bootlegged versions were either stolen or pirated. Either way, they had a perceived value.

One of my great pleasures during this phase of my life was to attend a weekly meeting of expat and local musicians who gathered together to play folk songs and generally busk around in a large local pub. I was under the impression that we got better and better as the night wore on. However, I had been having a dry February for many years, to prove to myself that I was not an alcoholic; most people try this in January, but I was of the view that if you are going to have a month off, you may as well make it the shortest month of the year. When February rolled around, I continued my attendance at the music sessions, but imagine my surprise when the noise we made became more raucous and rougher as the night went on. The Russians have an expression for this that sums up the pain involved – they say, 'an elephant stood on my ear'. In this case, it was an entire herd.

Smallbone and I reactivated our creative-writing collaboration by penning a few comic songs. Most of these have been lost to the mists of time, and just as well, because they were not as politically correct as they probably should have been. However, one week, a member of the folk club group asked me if we would be prepared to sing a couple of songs on live TV. I thought it was a wind-up, but the next Thursday while we were busily tanking up with beer, a TV van rolled up and four of us were bundled in to be taken to the studio. It suddenly dawned on me that this wasn't a practical joke, and we really were going on TV. The floor manager told us what to expect, and where to go when we walked on. Half an hour later, we were given the two-minute call in the green room. I bent down to pick up my guitar. Genc, a professional musician, put his hand gently on my shoulder. "Jack, tonight you must just sing. You're really shit at the guitar." All my illusions were shattered, but anyway I got my five minutes of fame singing the following comic song (translations/explanations of the Russian words in brackets were not sung).

Expats Don't Try to Learn Russian

As I was out walking Khreshchatyk one day

172

A man with a blue cap [a policeman] came waltzing my way

He said, you, sir, jaywalking, 'twill be bolshoi straf [a big fine]

I said, "Ne ponimayu" [I don't understand] – walked off with a laugh

Chorus:
Expats don't try to learn Russian
Translators when needed work grand
Don't try to arrest me – I just speak Englishki
Life is so sweet 'cos I don't understand

When I was out clubbing in Kiev one night
The queue to the club stretched to left and to right
Ignoring the catcalls, a terrible din
I said, "Ne ponimayu" – and then walked right in

Chorus

I was out driving my car with blue plates [diplomatic plate]

Wrong way down a one-way and other mistakes
The policeman said show me your license and such
I said, "Ne ponimayu" – and slipped in the clutch

Chorus

Taking a taxi to the airport one day
The price was three times what the locals would pay
Excuse me, druzhishche [buddy] – why do I pay more?
He said, "Ne ponimayu" – then slammed the door

Expats don't try to learn Russian
Translators when needed work grand
Come on then gouge me – I don't speak the lingi
We're all sitting ducks 'cos we don't understand.

The Kiev project finished all too quickly, and before I could really draw breath, my newly adopted company asked me if I could go to Kosovo for three months to prepare a nickel mine and smelter for privatisation. I knew nothing about privatisation, but how hard could it be?

Chapter 27: Kosovo – The Land That Time Forgot

"Do not go gentle into that good night,
Old age should burn and rave at close of day.
Rage, rage against the dying of the light." – Dylan Thomas

The land that is Kosovo has had a chequered history. I was flying into an area now under the control of the United Nations, supported by the armies of dozens of nations of the world. How did it come to this? A potted history, like the one I set out below, obviously misses the nuances and subtleties of such a complex history, but at least sets the scene.

1389 – The epic Battle of Kosovo heralds 500 years of Turkish Ottoman rule. Over the centuries, the religious and ethnic balance tips in favour of Muslims and Albanians.

1912 – Following the Balkan Wars, Serbia regains control of Kosovo from the Turks.

1946 – Kosovo is absorbed into the Yugoslav federation.

1974 – The Yugoslav constitution recognises the autonomous status of Kosovo, giving the province de facto self-government.

1990 – Yugoslav President Slobodan Milosevic strips Kosovo of its autonomy and imposes total Serbian administration on the territory, prompting Ibrahim Rugova to start a non-violent protest movement.

1991 – Start of the violent breakup of Yugoslavia. Kosovar Albanians launch a passive resistance movement but fail to secure independence.

1995 – The international community fails to act after the genocide of more than 8,000 Bosniaks (in Bosnia, rather than Kosovo of course). Later that year the Clinton administration in the US brokered the Dayton Accords, bringing the three-year Bosnian War to an end. Peace came only after the largest act of mass killing in Europe since World War II. However, while the agreement was successful in terminating the carnage in Bosnia, it failed to keep a check on Milošević and his repression of Kosovar Albanians.

Late 1990s – Clinton's jubilation at the signing of the Dayton Accords has unintended consequences, since it gave the impression that armed conflict would encourage the international community to intervene and resolve the situation sooner, creating what some have termed the moral hazard of humanitarian intervention.

1996 – The rebel Kosovo Liberation Army (KLA) steps up attacks on Serbian authorities in Kosovo. Their campaign grows, along with a brutal Serbian crackdown on the territory's Albanian population and by 1998 Kosovo was embroiled in a full-scale civil war.

1999 – After international efforts fail to stop the Kosovo conflict, NATO begins aerial bombardment of Serbian targets. Serbian forces respond with a campaign of ethnic cleansing against Kosovar Albanians, prompting an exodus of nearly 80 percent of the population. NATO troops enter Kosovo, driving back the Serbian military and following a hastily attained peace agreement, Serbian forces withdraw from Kosovo and a UN-sponsored administration takes over.

I arrived in Kosovo about eighteen months after the conflict had finished. There were troops and checkpoints everywhere manned by shaven-headed toughs, their arms held wide from their sides to accommodate bulging biceps (either that or they had razorblades in their armpits).

The Albanian Kosovars had been repressed for centuries and, once unleashed, their business acumen and flair enabled a lift in economic activity. This wasn't always well targeted; if someone had a good idea, everyone else piled in as quickly as they could, flooding the market.

One such business opportunity was the 'Auto Larje' (Car Wash). Anybody with fifty Euros for a pressure washer soon set up a small stand on the side of the road in Kosovo as a business. There were quite literally thousands of them. You can see the logic. In a place that belches black fumes from the brown coal-fired power stations, that contains vast numbers of home-based diesel generators, and that generally has high levels of dust and dirt, it didn't take too long for a car to get covered in grime. I always remember passing one forlorn car wash on an empty stretch of the road between Pristina and Peja. I never saw a single car being washed there and began to feel sorry for the guy trying to wave down the passing traffic. He did eventually come up with a genius idea. One day as I was passing, I saw a new sign: 'Tank Larje'. Sure enough, before long, he had a constant queue of tanks, all waiting their turn for a wash down.

The armies of NATO in Kosovo proved to be a microcosm of national stereotypes. Here is a completely unbiased, scientifically proven and empirical overview of these occupants from my ringside seat.

The Germans: Wonderful trucks and transports, very organised; their area is by far the most tidy and 'normal' looking in the country. They invest time in fixing things and repairing infrastructure. They get on well with the locals and generally have a good sense of humour. Lots of rules, but (unexpectedly) they are prepared to break them in order to make things work.

The Italians: Look flash and dashing, and have a load of expensive equipment, but you're never that certain that they actually know what to do with it. Incredible civil engineers (they replaced most of the bombed bridges in a matter of weeks). However, you see more of them drinking coffee in the pavement cafes than patrolling the streets. I couldn't make up my mind whether the crow's feather plumes they would stick in their hats looked charmingly unusual, or simply silly. Politically astute - they were originally scheduled to take over the Mitrovica area (of which more later), but they managed to convince the French to go there instead.

The French: Plenty of wonderful high-tech mobile equipment. Their mess is famous for being the best in Kosovo and the only army to routinely serve wine with the midday meal. Very organised when taking care of their own people and defending French interests, but basically couldn't give two hoots for anything else. They are in Mitrovica, the most difficult location – but I guess that serves them right for listening to the Italians.

The Americans: Loud, proud and supremely confident, and have more equipment than they know what to do with. Everything is big and brash – the trucks and Humvee vehicles are so large they have difficulty going down the narrow alleys. By far, the most intrusive military presence in Kosovo; when you're in the American sector, you really know it – there are flags, checkpoints and highly visible infantry formations everywhere. This said, they are also the most generous in terms of contracts with local businesses, which the local population greatly appreciate. Best 'PX' (NAAFI, if you're British) facilities in the country. Unexpectedly, the Americans are even more rule-bound than the Germans... there's a way for everything, and only that way is allowed (or so it seems).

The British: Next to all those big US trucks and flash Italian, French and German equipment, the British Land Rovers look rather quaint and retro. By far the best urban patrol troops in Kosovo (nice to know that all those years in Northern Ireland paid off); you hardly notice a British formation when they walk through town. Work hard at the 'hearts and minds' stuff, which the locals respond well to. Take a little too much delight in giving the French a hard time (the Royal Green Jackets sent an invitation to the head of the French division in Kosovo to attend their annual Waterloo Dinner).

And below a few equally scientific observations of some of the other twenty-odd military contingents:

The Norwegians: Great when they're sober. Even better when they're drunk.

The Greeks: Handle customs on the Macedonian border. Smoke on duty and shout a lot.

The Austrians: Have difficulty adjusting to how unlike Austria the whole place is.

The Indians: Lack modern equipment, but their eyeball-catching cornflower-blue camouflage fatigues make up for this by dazzling opponents into submission.

The Finns: Actually use mobile phones rather than radios for infantry communications. Every single one is called Haari.

The Swedes: Drive round in Volvos. All blond, blue-eyed and beautiful. I'm not sure how good they would be in a fight without their horned helmets these days though.

The Spanish: When two Spanish army drivers meet driving in opposite directions, army regulations require them to stop in the middle of the road to talk for ten minutes and smoke cigarettes.

The Portuguese: Become annoyed that everyone keeps asking them if they're Spanish. Maybe if they stopped doing that stop-in-the-middle-of-the-road thing, people would remember better.

The Russians: Talk to no one, spend most of their time 'borrowing' fuel for their trucks and can't stop resenting how much better off the other troops are.

The Ukrainians: Talk to no one, spend most of their time 'borrowing' fuel for their trucks and can't stop resenting how much better off the Russians are.

The three months' work I originally came to do was swiftly dealt with. Having made myself useful round the traps (and given that the first Director of Privatisation died of a heart attack whilst we were interviewing new staff), the grown-ups asked me to stay to help the new director settle in. Dick Dickson, the new guy, was a functional alcoholic who was brilliant at his job. He didn't turn up until the afternoon on any given day and so I was constantly covering for him. To be fair to Dick, he would then often work until 2am. If a man works to different hours, perhaps he sees a different clock; clearly, his was still in America. He made me his deputy, and this sealed my fate for the next five years.

Chapter 28: Privatisation

Turning something that was previously owned by the state into a privately owned something.

The Economist magazine introduced the term 'privatisation' or 'reprivatisation' (after the German *Reprivatisierung*) during the 1930s when it covered Nazi Germany's economic policy. It is not clear if the magazine coincidentally invented the word in English or if the term is simply a loanword from the same expression in German. The label may mean many different things, depending on the context. In my case, it meant stacking the sales shelves of the country's real estate supermarket with shiny socially owned assets as quickly as possible and selling them as swiftly as I could while garnering the least amount of hissing from the Germans.

In a balls-up typical to post-conflict projects, the privatisation agenda had been given to the US government, whilst economic reconstruction was led by the EU. This predictably led to an inevitable crisis, since the philosophical approach of the two donor organisations were poles apart. These two teams were to work together at the Kosovo Trust Agency (KTA) to implement a privatisation programme. Despite being a Brit, I was working with the US team who strongly believed that getting the 'socially-owned' assets into the private sector as quickly and efficiently as possible was the only way to effectively stimulate the economy. However, the Germans, the big guns in the EU team, were in favour of following the East German model in which assets were revitalized first and made fully functional before sale. As if this were not complex enough, the UN, who oversaw the whole shooting match, was only acting as an interim caretaker for owners as yet not quite defined, and further there had been partial privatisation of some assets in the past leaving a boat load of ownership claims. With so many snouts in the oversight trough, it was obvious why this was turning into such a pig's breakfast.

I always remember one of the first Germans arriving at the KTA. He was in his seventies and frankly was in an advanced stage of Alzheimer's. One of the first things he did was to declare the offices a smoking zone, and then proceed to chain-smoke large cigars. At the risk of sounding politically incorrect, the place became a gas chamber.

I found him on the stairs more than once, completely lost, and had to guide him to the gents, his office, or the external door. When we were having a 'get to know you' dinner, he turned to me and loudly declared, "You dropped bombs on me during ze war." You couldn't't make it up. He didn't last long, because even the feckless UN 'ne'er-do-anything' staffers worked out that this guy was a total liability. He was recalled to Berlin.

As an aside, the UN who were the directors of this mud-slinging fest between the EU and the US, adopted the default position of stopping anything with the slightest risk. After all, with that approach, you could not be held responsible for anything. So, even with the Alzheimer'sriddled apparatchik out of the way, the fight between the EU economic staff and the US privatisation staff continued to rage; while the UN apparatchiks did exactly what they normally do – precisely nothing.

This battle for the soul of privatisation raged for nearly two years. Dickson was thoroughly preparing the ground with processes and procedures, building regional teams and preparing detailed documentation for the sale of the assets. He was also waging a war, far too publicly, with the UN apparatchiks and, despite being warned time and time again to keep out of the press, he continued to write letters to the *Wall Street Journal* in his own name. While these letters (which always seemed to get published) were full of criticism and bile for the opposition, they were in my view completely accurate.

In the meantime, the lack of political and economic progress was making the Kosovar public increasingly restless. An incident in which some Albanian kids were forced into a river (rumour had it that they had been drowned) ignited an explosive set of riots that sent the region into total chaos. I went out on the streets at the time and saved myself from a certain beating on more than one occasion by holding my arms in the air and shouting at the top of my voice, "I'm American." I'd learned this technique from my buddy Thor, who had, in characteristic style, organised 'life's a riot' parties in downtown Pristina. Of course, I am not an American, but it had the desired effect –

the Kosovar Albanians are one of the few nations on Earth who do, totally and unreservedly, love Americans.

The UN had been completely taken by surprise by the riots and it took them two days to get a handle on the situation. The key was to cut off all mobile coms by turning off the phone towers, and to bring in the British SAS, who had good relationships with the KLA commanders. The British were able to persuade them to back off for the good of the future of Kosovo. It's my opinion that the lack of progress in economic development was a major reason for the unrest; the UN probably believed this too, as there was suddenly an urgent need to start the privatisation programme.

However, Dick had not learned my lesson about the truth setting you free; after the riots had calmed down, he continued to publicly castigate the UN and EU by writing letters to the mainstream media. The outcome was inevitable: he was given his marching orders. This left a vacuum for the Director of Privatisation post, and the EU desperately wanted their person in the role. The US head of mission was a feisty fellow, however, who was having none of it. The two sides came to a compromise; since I was European, but working for the Americans, I was offered the job – despite a total lack of qualifications and only two years of relevant experience during which time we had privatised stuff-all.

It was the first time in my life in which I had taken on a position in which the previous incumbent had done a brilliant preparation job. The UN was demanding fast action, and Dick had put us in such a state of readiness that all I needed to do was light the blue touch paper and we were away. What a fantastic job for a mining engineer – I was selling mines, quarries, breweries and vineyards, ski resorts, hotels and factories. It was less of a job and more of a pastime; after all, who wouldn't't enjoy showing investors round the country's breweries, with obligatory tastings and dinners? Life became a metaphorical riot for a while.

Chapter 29: Thor, God of Thunder

A ram retreats only to bring more power to the battle –
Nigerian Proverb

One of the delights of this sort of expatriate posting is the characters you meet and the friendships you make. One of the most charismatic men I have had the good fortune to work with was an American of Norwegian extraction by the name of Thor Hesla. He was to be the best man at my second wedding. He was also tragically murdered by the Taliban on 14th January, 2008. My wife and I, and a throng of other Thor pals, were waiting for him to join us for two weeks of skiing at Red Mountain in British Columbia when it happened, but that is another story.

Here is a eulogy by a friend of Thor's:

A Friend Called Thor

To some, it was his thirst for life; to others, his outsized personality, his humour, his unfailing, unconditional generosity. Yet whatever his many friends remember most about Thor Hesla, the Georgia native shot dead by a Taliban gunman in the gym of the Serena Hotel in Kabul in 2008, the world is a much poorer place without him.

To look at, he was all-American. He dressed in jeans, a checked shirt, a sleeveless fleece on very cold days and, when decorum required it, a tie – but only occasionally. His physique was a pear-shaped testament to two of his many loves: food and beer. He danced like a bear, rocking from one foot to the other, paws raised in the air.

He was very critical of the United States but loved it deeply. He once quipped that Americans used a Microsoft thought processor, but, in truth, his attitudes reflected the best of America. He was impatient with incompetence and hypocrisy; determined to find a better way to do things; certain that such a way existed. Above all, Thor was more than resilient; he was irrepressible. No-one with such a name could grow up to be a wallflower, and Thor could thunder when he wished. More often, he talked, articulately, volubly, and at length; slightly more assertive than required, but always incisive, and crystal clear in saying what he thought.

When Thor was murdered, the shock was twofold. Not just that anyone should die in such an attack; but that, of all the possible victims, Thor? It didn't ring true. In the natural order of things, he would be the first person to emerge from any disaster, the first to lead the recovery effort. And he would do a better job than anyone else. Indeed, amongst friends and colleagues the word 'Thorganise' came to signify extreme efficiency. But things don't always turn out as they should.

"A passionate believer" is how a CNN article described him shortly after his death. And he was, whether running domestic political campaigns for the Democratic Party, or promoting democracy overseas. When describing how he spent his 40th birthday working on a campaign in West Virginia, he wrote, "There was potential to be depressed: I was 40, all by myself, no family... but then I remembered: hey, I do this because I believe in elections and democracy and campaigns and the forum of ideas." He was far too intelligent, and irreverent, for simple dogma. He added: "And, of course, because campaigns afford me all kinds of goof-off time."

The Albanians have a saying that if you die leaving children, you only die a little, whereas, if you die without children, you die a lot. Thor was the exception that broke this rule, for despite being single and childless, thousands of people still keep his memory alive with celebrations of the life of our big Papa Bear.

In his early days in Kosovo, Thor penned this amusing and true story.

THE DWARF
I suppose if you live long enough, and in enough places, eventually everything pretty much happens to you. But if you had approached me in January 2003, and said, "Thor, in April you will be strangled by a dwarf in Pristina, Kosovo," I would have viewed you sceptically.

But it really happened the other day, and now I must tell you how. I am currently residing at the Hotel Baci, a very new facility with many of the perks of home, and a few of the charming twists which Pristina confers, like the perennial smell of diesel fumes from the generator which provides us with light and power for half the day and night when KEK, our hated national electricity utility, does not. But my employer will only give me a one-month stay there, so yesterday, about 11:00am, I was out looking at apartments, accompanied by Bujar, my trusty native guide, and Nezrit, a professional apartment hunter for UNMIK (the United Nations Mission in Kosovo).

After having emerged from the last of three, we were standing on a street corner, chatting amiably about the strengths and weaknesses of each of the apartments, when a sinister and menacing figure approached us.

Actually, not all that sinister and menacing, more like persistent and annoying. A cursory glance led me to the rapid impression that he was:

a) Romany

b) shorter than average

c) slightly hunchbacked

d) blessed with huge hands and an inordinately large forehead – but who am I to say he was a gypsy Mongoloid dwarf? I'm not a doctor, for God's sake!

He showed a striking grasp of English, thrusting one mitt the size of a baseball glove into the centre of our comradely circle and curtly snapping, "Gif me money."

Bujar and Nezrit gently demurred in fluid and polysyllabic Albanian, upon which he grew enraged and shouted, "Gif me money!" I elected to withdraw to the other side of the street. Unfortunately, just as I was about to disengage myself from this charming vignette, Beppo the Dwarf (remember that episode of *Frasier*?) lunged between Nezrit and Bujar and seized the lapels of my jet-black Nino Cerruti blazer.

"Gif me money!" he screamed.

"I say, old man," I sputtered, in my best Braxton-Migglesworth Eton/Oxford affected accent, "unhand me at once!"

Bujar and Nezrit proceeded to apply a flurry of KLA love-slaps, at which point Beppo significantly upped the ante by yanking me forward and hissing, "Gif me money, or I KILL you."

Hmmmm, thinks I to myself. Time to void the old sphincter? No, I decided, that just wouldn't be cricket!

Besides, it's 11:00 in the morning, a crowd is now starting to pay attention, and Bujar and Nezrit are sufficiently mobilised. What could go wrong. . .? And that's when my tie fell through my jacket and straight into Beppo's malevolent oven-mitts.

Quick as a wink, the little fucker latched on like a moray eel and proceeded to lift both my feet off the ground like I was the Great Bell of Notre Dame and he was some nasty little Romany Quasimodo. Of course, I was wearing a pretty nice tie, of Italian silk or something like that, and at that moment I realised why ties like that are popular for bondage: they're damned strong. Beppo's mouth was now next to my ear, I was almost doubled over, my tie (as ties will do, if tied appropriately) was cinching its way up to my larynx, and Beppo was hissing, over and over again, "Gif me money or I will KILL you."

NOW I was really thinking about soiling myself, but at that moment Beppo made a fatal mistake, which was to reposition his left hand on my tie ever so slightly, giving Nezrit, who was obviously an accomplished street grappler, the opening to apply the long-cherished LAPD combination wristlock/chokehold on the Beppster.

We proceeded to pummel our way free of Beppo, who loped off to sulk his way into some alley, and we retreated post-haste to the safety of Nezrit's car.

I sat in the back and fought to loosen my tie.

And that's when it hit me: I had been dwarf-strangled, in Kosovo.

Thor was the public relations manager in the Privatisation Department, and kept us both amused and organised. We had quite a few scrapes together, at one stage being mentioned in dispatches by the German Count in charge of the EU. Count, I said. The Count was demanding our immediate removal for allegedly stirring up ethnic tensions by putting out an advert for the sale of the Brezovica ski resort, located in a Serbian enclave. The Thorganiser had, of course, got sign-off from all the EU representatives, and produced this for the US Head of Mission who was carpeting us at the time. I had a déjà vu of the Magadan firing, with the authorities taking the easy option of removing us from the field of play, but to give the US Mission Head his due, he stood full-square behind us and the Count failed in his miserable plot to have us shot.

I remember another time when Thor and I were on our way down to Greece for the weekend, sharing a ride. This was a common weekend pursuit; we would eat copious quantities of food, drink generous volumes of Retsina and play frisbee in the warm Mediterranean waters under Mount Olympus. There was something fitting about Thor's thunderbolts that we could often observe from the beach. On this particular escapade, we were stopped by the cops on the road to the border in Kosovo for speeding. I was driving, but Thor insisted, "Don't worry, I'll do the talking." I deferred to him, thinking that maybe his silky tongue would get us off.

He wound down the window and the cop leaned in.

"Do you know why we stopped you?", he enquired.

"Well," said Thor, "we don't have doughnuts on the front seat, so it must be the coke in the trunk!"

Shit – there goes our weekend, I thought, images of a Pristina prison cell passing through my head. Fortunately, the cop was pretty laidback and realised Thor was fooling around.

"American, yes?" he half stated, half questioned. We nodded enthusiastically, and he waved us on with a mild admonition to slow down. The mental note I made to myself at the time was to never let Thor do the talking again... now I only wish he could.

Chapter 30: Ain't Life Grand

I'm their leader - which way did they go? - Alexandre Ledru-
Rollin

Apart from drunkenly singing a self-deprecating ditty live on Ukrainian TV, I have one other claim to fame and it centres on Pristina's Grand Hotel. The Grand was the subject of an article in the *Times* newspaper which called it the worst hotel in the world. British politician Chris Patten agreed, calling it "unbelievably grim." *Lonely Planet* included it "so that you don't get lured into staying", and the *In Your Pocket* guide wound up its review with, "We suggest demolition." Can any hotel really be that bad?

The 1999 war and Kosovo's limbo status as a country barely a third of the world recognised, had left Pristina brutalised. Right at the centre of the concrete cityscape was the thirteen-storey Grand Hotel, a 370-room monstrosity built in 1978 to accommodate Tito's communist cadres.

I took a visit to the bomb target to assess its potential. This was a long way from Kosovo's lovely valleys, the old Ottoman town of Prizren or the idyllic Mirusha waterfalls. All you could see from the thirteenth-floor window were the palls of black smoke from the power station in the distance. Looking down you could see the derelict shopping centre – too scary even for graffiti artists. Where the scree of debris ended, dozens of pristine white UN vehicles were corralled in a car park surrounded by barbed wire.

A brief inspection of the rooms revealed threadbare green carpets and broken bathtubs with basins even Mrs Orme would have condemned. The TripAdvisor guide noted that "Two of us had to get medical treatment because of bugs in the mattresses." I gave up on the tour of the rooms and decided to try the food on offer. In the vast dining hall, there were three chandeliers each sporting a Christmas tree of grey dust bearing globes one or two glimmering feebly like the last coals of a camp fire, a hundred empty tables and two grumpy staff. One, a lady sitting at a central table as if supervising an exam, stabbed her pen into a ledger to get my attention. I gave my name and a flourish of her heavily braceleted wrist told me to move on. The buffet was boiled eggs, cheese slices, tomatoes and coffee. Both staff watched me fumble with the coffee machine but didn't offer any assistance. I picked disconsolately at the feast and soon decided to leave before food poisoning set in and I would need to inspect the toilets. Ledger lady shot me an intimidating stare, and her male colleague marched to the door. He got there just ahead of me and, with his arms tightly folded and feet planted apart, bouncer-style, barred my exit. I froze. He was terrifying. What could I have done wrong?

He looked down at me sternly, like an interrupted genie, "Haff nice day," he said, then moved sideways, just enough to let me pass. He'd been on a customer-service course, apparently. I don't think he'd quite got the point.

My claim to fame in all this is that I managed to sell this monstrosity, "the Worst Hotel in the World" for eight million euros!

I spent five wonderful years in Kosovo as director of privatisation and sold 600 million euros worth of assets, effectively selling most of the country's businesses right up to the declaration of independence. I then devoted another year, post-independence, advising the government of the newest country in the world. The economy did take off once the socially owned business were transferred to private hands. Today, Pristina is an attractive buzzing city and I feel quite warm inside that I helped this to happen. There is, of course, a tinge of sadness that corruption crept into the system. I once noted to the then Prime Minister, Ramush Haridinaj (fondly referred to as Rambo by those who know him well), that Kosovo had been ranked third from bottom on the world's corruption index. He replied that there was thus still something to aim for. I am still not quite sure what he meant by that.

There were some other amusing vignettes. As the country stabilised and became less tense after independence, the race was on to get as many countries around the world as possible to recognise the newly independent state. UNMIK started to reduce troop numbers. One day I was invited to the Peja encampment of the Spanish military to observe the handover as the Spanish withdrew. It's notable that, due to their own issues with the Basque and Catalan independence movements, that the

Spanish government was unwilling to acknowledge Kosovo's independence from Serbia. I remember clearly that, at the handover ceremony, the mayor of Peja clasped the Spanish commander in a mawkish bearhug, like a long-lost brother. The Spanish commander enquired as to why he was so pleased to see him, given Spain's stance on recognition.

"That's OK," said the mayor. "You discovered America, and that is good enough for me."

Chapter 31: Leaving Kosovo

"Friendship is like wet cement - the longer you stay the harder it is to leave, and the deeper the footprint you leave behind." – Khaled Hishma

After a longer time than I had spent anywhere, ever, it was time to move on, and back into the mining industry proper. My friends and colleagues arranged a goodbye dinner for me. This is the speech I gave at that occasion:

"Friends... After six years in Kosovo, there comes a time to say farewell... And when saying something at such gatherings I am reminded of something Plato said: "Wise men talk because they have something to say. Fools talk because they have to say something..."

With that in mind, I will keep this speech brief. It is interesting to think that over my forty-eight years of life, Kosovo is the place that I have spent the longest time... and the reason for this is that it has been the most intensely interesting and professionally challenging country I have had the pleasure to live in, and the most personally fulfilling. You, my friends and I, achieved a great deal... freeing most of the assets tied down by the yoke of Yugoslav socialism into the private sector – lighting the fire of new investment and leaning forward towards independence...

I am now, probably for the first time in my life, the person I have always wanted to be. Not my physical body! I despair over that – the wrinkles, the baggy eyes and the sagging belly. Often I am taken aback by that fat, ageing man that lives in my mirror, but I won't agonise over those things now.

I would never trade my amazing friendships – forged over the last six years of challenges – my wonderful life or the memories of the great people I have worked with, the things they have achieved to make this country and therefore this world a better place... No, I wouldn't trade the memories of my friendships for less wrinkles or a flatter belly. I don't chide myself for eating and drinking too much or for buying an extra pair of skis I don't really need, but that look so avant-garde in my hall. For I have seen too many dear friends leave this world too soon; before they understood the great freedom that comes with age and experience. Now, I know our Kosovar friends like an anecdote... and I felt this a good moment to retell a couple that I told to the graduating class of the Professional Development Program a couple of years back... will those graduates please forgive the retelling... They are stories of Moral Courage...

Many years ago, Al Capone owned Chicago. Capone wasn't famous for anything heroic. He was notorious for enmeshing the Windy City in everything from bootlegged booze and prostitution to murder.

Capone had a lawyer nicknamed Easy Eddie. He was his lawyer for good reason. Eddie was very good! In fact, Eddie's skill at legal manoeuvring kept Big Al out of jail for a long time. To show his appreciation, Capone paid him very well. Not only was the money big, but Eddie received special dividends. For instance, he and his family occupied a fenced-in mansion with live-in help and all of the conveniences of the day. Eddie lived the high life of the Chicago mob and gave little consideration to the corruption that went on around him.

Eddie did have one soft spot, however. He had a son that he loved dearly. Eddie saw to it that his young son had the best of everything: clothes, cars and a good education. Nothing was withheld. Price was no object. Despite his involvement with organised crime, Eddie tried to teach him right from wrong. Eddie wanted his son to be a better man than he was. Yet, with all his wealth and influence, there were two things he couldn't give him; he couldn't pass on a good name or a good example.

One day, Easy Eddie reached a difficult decision. He wanted to rectify the wrongs he had done. He decided he would go to the authorities and tell the truth about Al 'Scarface' Capone, clean up his tarnished name and offer his son some semblance of integrity. To do this, he would have to testify against the mob, and he knew that the cost would be great. But he testified.

Within the year, Easy Eddie's life ended in a blaze of gunfire on a lonely Chicago street. But in his eyes, he had given his son the greatest gift he had to offer, at the greatest price he would ever pay. Police removed from his pocket a poem clipped from a magazine. The poem read:

The clock of life is wound but once
And no man has the power
To tell just when the hands will stop
At late or early hour.
Now is the only time you own.
Live, love, toil with a will.
Place no faith in time.
For the clock may soon be still.

The second story is the story of a World War II hero, Lieutenant Commander Butch O'Hare. He was a fighter pilot assigned to the aircraft carrier *Lexington* in the South Pacific.

One day his entire squadron was sent on a mission. After he was airborne, O'Hare checked his fuel gauge and realised that someone had forgotten to top off his fuel tank. He would not have enough fuel to complete his mission and return to his ship. His flight leader told him to go back to the carrier. Reluctantly, he dropped out of formation and headed back to the fleet. As he was returning to the mothership he saw something that turned his blood cold – a squadron of enemy aircraft were speeding their way toward the American flotilla.

The American fighters were gone on a sortie, and the fleet was all but defenceless. He couldn't reach his squadron and bring them back in time to save the fleet. Nor could he warn the fleet of the approaching danger. There was only one thing to do. He must somehow divert the enemy aircraft.

Laying aside all thoughts of personal safety, he dived his aircraft into the formation of enemy planes. Wing-mounted fifty-calibres blazed as he charged in, attacking one surprised enemy plane and then another. Butch weaved in and out of the now broken formation and fired at as many planes as possible until all his ammunition was finally spent.

Undaunted, he continued the assault. Diving at the planes, trying to clip a wing or tail in the hope of damaging as many enemy aircraft as possible and rendering them unfit to fly.

Finally, the exasperated enemy squadron took off in another direction. Deeply relieved, Butch O'Hare and his tattered fighter limped back to the aircraft carrier. Upon arrival he reported in and related the events surrounding his return. The film from the gun-camera mounted on his plane told the tale.

It showed the extent of Butch's daring attempt to protect his fleet. He had in fact destroyed five enemy aircraft. For his actions Butch became the Navy's first Ace of World War II, and the first naval aviator to win the Congressional Medal of Honor. A year later Butch was killed in aerial combat at the age of twenty-nine. His hometown would not allow the memory of this war hero to fade, and today, O'Hare International Airport in Chicago is named in tribute to the courage of this great man.

If you find yourself at O'Hare International, give some thought to visiting Butch's memorial, displaying his statue and his Medal of Honor. It's located between Terminals 1 and 2.

So, what do these two stories have in common?

Butch O'Hare was Easy Eddie's son. In many ways these stories are a reflection of the Kosovo we find ourselves in today. Previously deeply flawed but now presented with a fresh canvas on which to paint a new inspiring democracy. I implore you my good friends to grab the opportunity that faces you to continue to build your new country with the same courage and integrity that Butch displayed.

To wrap up this speech, a Kosovar VIP said something to me recently that gave me pause for thought. He asked me if I had anything to be ashamed of during my time in Kosovo. I was taken aback for I truly believe that we had done our level best to make the country a better place, and that I, and the people I have had the honour to work with, had toiled with honesty and integrity. Sure, we made mistakes, but honest mistakes are what give us strength, understanding and compassion. Those making no decisions at all will never know the joy of daring to fail, of risking all in the pursuit of a new democracy. For imperfection is the child of honest actions. So, I told him the only thing I can think of is that I am ashamed to admit is... that I really like ABBA songs.

I am incredibly happy to have spent enough time in Kosovo to have my youthful laughs be forever etched into the grooves on my face. To today's Kosovo, I wish you a day of ordinary miracles, of moral courage, and I thank you for your friendship, your understanding and your kindness. And with this I say not goodbye but *au revoir*, secure in the knowledge that we will meet again."

During my Kosovo days, I had bought a dilapidated farmhouse in the Pyrenees, and it was to this that my wife and I moved next, full of plans for renovation, including the building of a pub. After about six months on the construction tools, it dawned on me that at some stage the cash would run out. An old mining analyst buddy called me up just as I was reaching this conclusion. I set off to London with two pasties and a packet of ginger nuts in my pocket to meet with two Russians, who were looking for a CEO to drive through an IPO. This sounded like an entertaining project and, given that they clearly knew stuff-all about mining, it was bound to be somewhat interesting.

Chapter 32: Iron Fist Ltd

"Psu pod hvost", is a Russian saying, literally meaning 'under a dog's tail'. In essence, whatever was done went to waste, had no effect or was pointless.

I met Boris Popka in Claridges. This move was clearly designed to impress me, and it worked. A good interview over lunch was followed by a second interview a week later with Lev Brilentine. We agreed to join forces to work towards an IPO on the AIM market in London. As I dug deeper into the details of the project, I began to sense that this was not going to be as easy as I'd first thought.

Unquestionably, there were some definite major plus points. The orebody was located just 7km from the Trans-Siberian railway and therefore within cheap transport of four major steel smelters. The company also had about 50,000 metres of drill core from its previous geological campaigns. Despite the project site being located in deepest Russia, the fact that they had a good friend of Putin on the board (indeed someone who had worked closely with him during his formative years) gave a degree of credibility to our ability to operate. The ground where the orebody is located was thankfully free of villages and towns while also having good access to both power and roads. Of course, there are always downsides as well. In this case, the ore itself was only running about 35 percent iron, and although there was nearly a billion tonnes of it, it would need a massive processing plant to upgrade the ore to a saleable 60 percent. Further, the orebody was flat, about 80 to 100 metres thick, and some 600 metres below the surface. As a result, this would have to be an underground operation and so would need a couple of billion dollars to develop.

The first step was to identify the right brokers. Getting back into the City of London was going to prove trickier than I would have liked for the puritanical winds of 2008 were stilling chilling the investment community. We put a detailed presentation together and started making the rounds of the broking houses.

I knew things were not going to be pretty when, close to the end of a meeting with the mining team of a large bank, Boris threw the first of his incendiary rages in my presence, on the subject of valuation. By this point in my life, I had witnessed a good deal of aggression, anger, fights and fallouts, but this one took fury to new heights. He strode around the room like a wounded lion, swearing and cussing at the top of his voice, smashing his phone to pieces on the conference table and glaring murderously – from six inches away - into the bank team's faces, all the while still spitting chips. I was deeply embarrassed. I got up quietly, left the room, went to the underground station and took the tube to Heathrow. What else could I do? To me, it was all over. At home in France I read the email from the offended banker. While he didn't place any blame at my door, he assured me that he wouldn't be doing business with us. Another nail in the coffin of a project I had already mentally buried. I assumed that this coffin had been lowered into the hole of a grave marked WTF!?

About two weeks later, I received a call from Boris, full of apologies, asking me to come back and resurrect the process. I wasn't keen, but when he assured me that he would let me do all the talking, I (foolishly) relented. After all, beggars can't be choosers and I needed something to fill the empty war chest.

We resumed the round of brokers. Despite the mining finance world being a small one, we managed to get two fairly large broking houses to take us on. We took the brokers' analysts out to kick the tires of the asset, completed a Scoping Study with DARK consultants, took on a leading law firm and put together a pathfinder document. We then ran around the City doing a dog and pony show, whilst building to book (a process whereby the brokers obtain promises of a certain level of investment at a defined price).

We were looking for about $45 million. Boris and Lev had insisted on a valuation of the assets at $220 million. I knew this was a bit on the cheeky side, but I hoped that as we built the book, we could talk them down off this perch. How wrong I was.

I had been invited to have dinner at the Popka household and as we were chewing the verbal cud in the kitchen before actually eating, I confronted Boris with the fact that we had received promises for $20 million based on a valuation of $120 million, he started to turn a little pink. Thinking that this was the time to press on and finish what I knew would be an awkward conversation, I expressed the idea that if we dropped the valuation to $100 million, we would get the total $45 million raise away, when I noticed his fist starting to clench. Then his jaw started clenching rhythmically and his lips peeled back, baring teeth like an angry Rottweiler. His face turned purple as the final wave of rage hit him. I was undoubtedly witnessing an imminent volcanic eruption and took cover. He found the only thing he could get his hands on, a roast chicken that had just come out of the oven, and started to rip it to pieces with his bare hands, burning himself in the process as he launched chicken body parts in random directions. I had learned from the first episode that he became so full of rage that he didn't notice other people. I slipped out, bidding farewell to his lovely wife and children in the hall, and then made my way back out to the tube and took the route back to the airport for a flight to France. I made another mental note to self, save the bad news until after the pudding, I was bloody starving.

I had a long chat with the brokers the next morning to see whether there was any flexibility on the price. There wasn't. Two days later, I spoke with Boris, who was still seething, but who had regained the power of coherent speech. I don't know what the real story was, or who was actually behind the project (I sensed that he was following orders) but he wouldn't budge from his desired valuation. I told him I was out of the project and that I couldn't help them any further.

About three months later, he approached me again. Could I help him sell the project for the $100 million price tag? Who would have thought it? I was willing to give it a shot, of course, and spent a month working with the brokers looking for a trade sale. Same story. The trade buyer was only willing to pay up to $60 million. Rage, toys thrown out of the pram, dummy spat, complete with gnashing teeth. I walked away for the third and (I am pleased to say) final time.

Greed is of course common in the City. However even in a place where it is so entrenched, Boris managed to take greed to new heights. My one piece of advice to anyone looking to raise money is to be prepared to leave a chunk of value on the table for the new investor - otherwise why would they bother to put their money in? The company and assets were eventually sold on to a local Russian company at a price never disclosed to me. I would bet good money that it was less than the $60 million.

I never received any payment from the company for the many months of work I had put in. Needless to say, this contributed to my somewhat cynical view of promoters and other City slickers, always wanting something for nothing.

Smallbone was calling and he had the perfect short-term job for me, advising the mining ministry in Afghanistan. Needs must where the devil drives and, reluctantly, I took it.

Chapter 33: Mission Kabul... Mission Impossible

"We all hoped in 2001 that we could put in place an Afghan government under President Karzai that would be able to control the country, make sure al-Qaeda didn't come back, and make sure the Taliban wasn't resurging. It didn't work out." – Colin Powell

For some reason my parents were a little concerned when I told them I was heading to Afghanistan, so once I had arrived, I wrote to reassure them:

Dear Mum and Dad,

Kabul is a very strange place. In essence, it's an enormous prison with thousands upon thousands of bearded heavies guarding big villas with Kalashnikovs. The police and military patrol the streets like ants awaiting a visit from an anteater. They scurry about with a passionate intensity, and when you traverse Kabul, it is not unusual to catch furtive looks checking you out from dark alleys or the corners of buildings. The traffic is in an almost permanent state of citywide gridlock every time I have to travel anywhere and the potholes in the roads have now grown so large that they are practically quarries themselves. Hence the need for some mining advice, no doubt. The traveller is definitely shaken not stirred.

I live, if that is what it can be called, in a villa shared

with eight other convicts. The villa is protected by a 20-foot-high concrete wall with a razor-wire fence on top and Gurkhas who are carrying stupefyingly big guns.

Entry to the compound requires the gate guard to peer through a small window and check mirrors reflecting the street outside. The guard then opens an outer metal door and the potential entrants step into a cage constructed of chain link fencing and sturdy metal poles. The guarding Gurkhas' gimlet eyes scrutinise 'intruders' as the outer door is locked, training their rifles on the cage from three strategically located foxholes. Silent nods between the guard team allow the door on the inner cage to be opened and the short walk to the front door of the villa is then permitted.

Each time I need to move from one designated safe place to another, I have an armed escort. To achieve such a move, a warrior with an automatic rifle, a sidearm and an expression that would freeze boiling oil keeps me company as our armoured vehicle navigates the craters. His expression is probably the scariest thing – it scares the bejesus outa me, anyway.

My chances of being killed, kidnapped or injured are slight given the multiple levels of defence, and would be down to unluckily being in the wrong place at the wrong time. Indeed, my theory concerning Thor's death is that he was mistaken for the Norwegian ambassador who was resident in the Serena hotel, and therefore became a high-profile target as an accident of mistaken identity. The insurgents are not really going after lowly economic consultants like us, I am assured, but they are notoriously bad shots. The real risks are getting in the way of an off-target RPG or being caught in the crossfire in a place where there are VIPs who they are targeting. Fortunately for me, I am an extremely small cog in the big machine, and I don't hobnob with the big knobs.

So, I think I'll be alright. Love Jack xxx

I received by return a short missive stating, "Your grandfather was an officer in the Gurkhas. You're safe. Dad xxx"

At first sight Gurkhas are not all that impressive. They are short and lean with an implacable expression that masks a determination and bravery which is second to no other soldier. The British army managed to defeat them in 1816 but only because the Nepalese were so overstretched fighting with the Chinese and Tibetans at the same time. They also had the very minor technological disadvantage of fighting with swords against guns. The Brits, always up for a scrap, quickly came to the conclusion that they needed these guys on their side and wrote a treaty to co-opt them. The Gurkhas have fought gallantly in every major British battle ever since.

Gurkhas have no fear. They follow a cultural system of 'Kaida' which requires an unquestionable loyalty to officers and to each other. The commanding officer of a Gurkha dying in pain on the battlefield was told that his man would only survive if he had the will to live. As the Gurkha slipped into unconsciousness, the officer barked an order at him to live and, needless to say, the man revived and lived to fight another day. The Gurkha regiment has received more medals than any other, and 99 percent of its recruits complete the maximum twenty-two-year tenure of service. This is a higher percentage than any other army or regiment in the world and is a testament to their steely makeup. The British, having retained the Gurkhas' indispensable services, added rifles and grenades to their weaponry to create, arguably, the most obdurate fighting machine in the world.

The Gurkha sword is called a Kukri, and by tradition once drawn it must taste blood. If the enemy sensibly runs away, surrenders or dies prior to the required tasting, the Gurkha will cut himself before sheathing the blade. I was indeed protected, for no one comes close to the Gurkha in the badass department.

There was a gym in the villa which I had, against all odds, started using every day. I cycled gently away with the stationary bike on freewheel whilst watching the BBC World Service, providing myself with the self-deluding impression that I was getting fit. The three scary-looking Gurkhas, whose mission was to protect us whilst within the house, usually lurked in the gym. They'd march around stealthily, musclebound and looking like thin sacks stuffed full of walnuts. When I entered the gym, they would all utter a respectful but undeserved, "Sir", salute and then retire discreetly to their quarters. I'd secretly drop off the weights and resistances on the gym machines to a minimum, only to max them up again before I left. I vainly hoped that they might be impressed when they returned to re-occupy the gym. A great deal of my time was spent incarcerated in the villa, but I tried not to spend too long hogging the gym – I needed these guys to be as fit as possible in case something did go down.

Every weekday morning, we would meander our way to the Ministry of Mines. One day I was in the back of an armoured Landcruiser heading into the city. I felt modestly safe. Although the traffic was crawling at about 15 kph, it was at least still moving. Suddenly, the traffic jammed up and my driver slammed on the brakes. The donkey cart behind us didn't have the same braking capability, and the face of the donkey crashed into the rear window with a sickening thump. Snot and a donkey-face-shaped print smeared the glass, and pandemonium ensued; my driver floored the accelerator and mounted the curb, sending pedestrians sprawling for cover as we sped away from the scene like bank robbers. I understood that my protection team thought this might be an attack. I personally think that ramming cars with donkeys isn't quite the weapon of mass destruction we all fear, but you never know.

On the rare occasions I did get out of the villa, designated safe spaces were limited and sometimes surprising. There were the obvious places, such as the government ministries, but also a 'tea' shop which only served wine in teapots, to be drunk from the finest porcelain cups. Afghanistan has a Muslim constitution and is supposedly teetotal, but that particular establishment has interpreted the rules with a delicate finesse. A pot of 'French tea' cost sixty dollars and was the most noxious, blood-coloured slightly alcoholic swill it's been my unfortunate need to imbibe.

On my first tour of duty, I had discovered that the customs guys X-ray all bags coming into the country. On approaching the machine, I wondered who would be nuts enough to bring drugs into the heroine-growing capital of the world and a place where hemp grows profusely on the plains. I was somewhat disgruntled when they spotted my three bottles of fine Bordeaux wine on the screens and confiscated them. However, needs must where the Taliban ride, and so I became a weekly visitor to the tea shop. Most likely to drink my own confiscated wine.

My job involved writing a strategy paper on the extractive industries for Afghanistan. Sadly, this required very little interaction with local people, though the ones I met at the Ministry of Mines were delightful and friendly. One of the joys of this sort of mission is to engage with the local culture and get to understand and share diverse perspectives, but there was little opportunity to learn much about the locals' lives on this one. The expats were good-willed, but odd, and in my villa there was limited social interaction. They sure would have been safe from the Covid-19. The advisors would come through the cage, up the steps and through the front door, go straight to the kitchen, take food from the buffet laid out, microwave it, and retire to their rooms to eat, sleep or work. The long-termers seemed loath to interact with new blood. The few expatriates I did spend time with fell into three basic camps: Missionaries, Mercenaries and Misfits.

Missionaries: all the zeal, no real idea and here to save the world, hurrah!

Mercenaries: fighting yet another economic or social war... for cash, of course, and

Misfits: the eccentrics and oddballs, the flotsam and jetsam that always seem to wash up someplace strange and settle in.

My first tour was rather boring, but I didn't quite lose the will to live. On my next visit, to overcome the inconvenience and cost of drinking alcoholic drain cleaner, I loaded up with wine boxes. This fooled the X-ray operators and made me more popular than pork scratchings at the Cannabis Cup festival with my fellow villa dwellers.

Alcohol appeared to be the grease that loosened tongues and opened the souls of the waifs and strays who wandered into this dangerous dead end. The mercenaries, missionaries and misfits suddenly warmed up a bit, once plied with the finest vintage boxed plonk.

Where did I fit into all this, I wondered? I needed to mull that one over a bit. Maybe 'Kabul Jack' was a mixture of all three character types... Actually, 'Kabullshit Jack' seems to fit the bill rather better...

Chapter 34: Miracle Muck

'A gold mine is a hole in the ground surrounded by liars' -
Mark Twain

After Afghanistan I undertook a number of other short-term assignments in order to keep the wolf from the door. One of my small projects was a two-week trip to Morocco to review a number of mineral prospects for an Australian fund manager who I worked for on a regular basis. Morocco is nothing like the romantic image painted in the film *Casablanca*. It's a heady mix of French and Arab culture – with the most challenging aspects of each of them. Indeed, in my somewhat limited experience, I found the people I worked with to be idlers, loafers and dodgers, economic with the truth, heavy with repurposed facts, and with an ability to test one's incredulity to the limit. I guess in the world of Trump, this is no longer a notable issue, since truth and facts are mostly inconvenient. Indeed, I understand that Trump was caught telling the truth the other day, but of course he denied it.

This job manifested itself in one of the more interesting moments of my entrepreneurial life. At the insistence of my guide, Mr. Whato, I travelled about 1500 km to meet with two individuals who, I was assured, would make my associates and me as rich as Croesus. We travelled for hours and hours over dusty, potholed roads. Just as I was beginning to lose the will to live, a grubby, dishevelled little hotel fell into view.

"This is it," said Whato with mounting excitement. Indeed, it was. Having sold the 'worst hotel in the world', I think myself something of an expert in bad hotels. This one felt like the end of the world. If it wasn't the end of the world, it could probably be seen from there. I am, of course, always willing to suspend belief, but this didn't bode well for a new partnership with the wealthy Moroccan joint venture partners I had been promised.

We checked in, and I washed the engrained grime of the day's travel from my tired, shaken body. I repaired to the bar for a cool, refreshing beer to cleanse the dust from my insides. Whato was there, already three pints down. I took that first delightful gulp of the amber nectar just as Whato burst into a delighted yelp, leaping from his chair to greet two disconsolate-looking fellows.

One was about five foot two, the other around six foot four. Whato, having greeted them effusively, introduced them. We swapped pleasantries, and the small one launched into what must have been a prepared speech. He and his partners were masters of the locality: they could open any door, they could secure any project, they could move any mountain. I noted dryly that we were looking for gold exploration projects.

"Gold exploration projects," he proclaimed. "You have come to the right people." He gestured to his partner with both hands. "Abdul can smell gold when its buried under twenty meters of basalt."

I thought for a split second. "Great, let's just suspend him beneath a helicopter and fly him round till we find something."

To my amazement, they took this suggestion completely seriously. I had been beginning to think that I had seen it all, but clearly there was still more madness out there.

Another small project was a six-month stint in Kyrgyzstan. I found the people of this republic to be the most laidback and zen I had ever worked with. The Chief of Party couldn't believe how small the mining world was as I kept running into people I knew, or people who knew people I knew. I made a bet with her that if I could find someone in common with any mining person I met within two minutes, she would buy me a shot, and if I couldn't I would buy her one. I only bought her one shot in my time there.

One of the great joys of this type of work is discovering new cities. I loved the green and verdant parks in Bishkek. Karaoke machines set about ten metres apart lined the paths, enabling hundreds of competing crooners to battle it out with assaults on your eardrums.

The work was interesting. The Minister of Mines wanted to make the country more attractive for inward investment. His plan was to develop a more attractive mining law, and then use this as a promotional tool.

Kumtor, the world's highest gold mine, represented about 40 percent of the country's GDP, but it was a one-trick pony, and he wanted to develop more Kumtors. I set about analysing the situation. With the aid of some great local sleuths in the project team, we stepped through the entire process from getting permission to look for minerals, to discovery, and then the subsequent development of a mine. Slowly and painstakingly, we mapped out a chart of all of the steps needed, identifying the responsible ministries and departments for each permit. The minister came in to see our progress just as we had completed this gargantuan task.

"So, what do you think, Jack, would you invest here?", he enquired.

I rolled out the chart, which was twenty pages of A4 taped together, which mapped out the key milestones in the process.

"There are a hundred and sixty-one permits typically required to be obtained from five different ministries. As soon as anyone does their due diligence on the legals, they will keep running 'til they're out of the 'stans."

He was shocked. However, together with the ministry staff we spent a lot of time simplifying the laws and regulations, and created a 'one-stop shop' to give potential investors the possibility of obtaining all their licenses from a dedicated and highly skilled team of locals. I would like to note that Kyrgyzstan is a great place to end up, especially if you like karaoke.

Chapter 35: Mining Entrepreneur

"Entrepreneurs: The only people who work 80-hour weeks to avoid working 40-hour weeks for someone else, and for half the pay." – Lori Greiner

After a few of these jaunts checking out some of the less travelled corners of the planet, I was now on a break, hanging out at home base in France. I was counting down the days to the start of the European skiing season when an old buddy from Australia, Louis Pilier, called me up. He told me that he was coming to Europe to give a presentation at a conference. Louis had become a fund manager in Sydney and had three days to kill before the conference – did I want to hang out? "Come on down," I said. What could possibly go wrong?

I picked Louis up at Toulouse airport and we headed south to the Pyrenees, catching up on old times. It was great to see an old mate, and we talked and talked and talked about the old days at the Isa. I learnt that a number of our former colleagues from those times had become extraordinarily wealthy and, oddly enough, not those who had been predicted to do so.

He had an idea to start a new company focused on antimony, a metalloid the research indicated would come into increasing demand. Antimony has been used historically as an additive to ordnance, to make lead harder, and as a medical purgative. Concerning this last use, there are only four antimonial cups still in existence: one of them belonged to Sir Francis Drake and can be viewed in the Victoria and Albert Museum in London. The user would pour his wine into the cup and drink it twenty-four hours later, which seems like a hellishly long time to wait for a sip. It would, I am reliably informed, completely clear the pipes in the human waste management system. There were also antimony pills which had much the same effect when swallowed. I don't know quite how they recovered the pill at the end of the process, but I suspect that's why you don't find too many of those either.

These days, antimony is predominantly used as a fire retardant in plastics and as an additive to the lead plates in acid batteries. It is also used in optical glass and as a catalyst in the production of plastic bottles. What excited Louis and I was the fact that both the US Geological Survey and the European Union Geological Survey had identified antimony as the metal most at risk of supply disruption on a global scale. Add to this its new potential uses as large-scale liquid metal batteries, and its special characteristics that have enabled the development of even faster phase change memory (that's the memory card in your 'phone), and you could see why we got a little carried away.

I took him up to the Balnea spa in the mountains; it was late November and there were a few flurries of snow. The series of outdoor Japanese pools run from thirty-six to forty degrees Celsius and are the ideal place to chill out and enjoy the splendid mountain scenery, while you slowly cook like a lobster in a cauldron.

Louis was far more connected with our former colleagues from the Isa than I was, given his base in Australia. It seemed that the guys who had become so wealthy had all also mentally regressed to being teenagers with their infallibility complexes and an absolute sense of entitlement, believing that the sun shone from their soil pipe. If truth be told, those who had made it financially had all become wankers.

"Shoot me if I become a wanker," I said.

And with that our company was born and I was about to embark on the next phase of my career as a mining entrepreneur. The initials SMIIBAW Ltd, were registered in Australia and we promised each other that we would keep the real meaning (**S**hoot **M**e **I**f **I** **B**ecome **A** **W**anker) out of circulation. But there were many a slip between cup and lip, and first close friends and then an ever-widening group, came to know its meaning.

Louis tipped some cash into the company and we ran around the world, raising funds and snapping up antimony projects wherever we could find them, all the while making presentations at numerous conferences. It was a blast. When things really started to get serious – that is, after we had identified a stranded asset in South Africa – it became clear from the sniggering of our usually sour-faced accountants that we needed to change the name. Reluctantly we changed it to Stibium Mining: Stibium being the Latin word for antimony (its chemical symbol on the periodic table is Sb).

That stranded asset, the Cons Murch mine in South Africa, was an old mine with a venerable history dating back to the 1930s. It had the largest known resource of antimony in the world and was therefore of immense interest to Stibium. We made an indicative offer to Village Main Reefs, the company who owned it, and managed to get a three-month exclusivity period. We visited the site several times during our due diligence work. It was clear that management had lost the support of the workforce and that, without a capital injection, the mine was going downhill fast. However, raising the much needed capital for the revitalisation was proving difficult. We had to spend the first twenty minutes of any meeting or presentation explaining what antimony was, and why it was important. One interesting characteristic of antimony is that it is nearly always found close to gold, and the Cons Murch orebodies were no exception. Antimony was averaging roughly 1.8 percent in the orebodies with gold running at 2 grams a tonne. There were gold-rich areas and antimony-rich areas. This had allowed the mine to switch focus as relative metal prices fluctuated. It also meant that areas with an abundance of one metal had sometimes been abandoned in time of low prices and forgotten. There were some exciting opportunities to investigate.

On one trip, I asked to have a meeting with the unions on the mine. With great reluctance, the General Manager,

Mr. Foursquare, arranged it. The three union representatives trooped into the boardroom: two from the NUM, one from Solidarity and one from UASA. I stared hard at a portly fellow with an enormous Father Christmas beard and flecks of white curly hair. The face looked familiar. He stared back at me.

"I know you," he observed.

"Kloof?" I said.

"Ah, it's that lanky streak of piss Englishman who couldn't turn up of a morning."

"Not so streaky anymore," I retorted, "Boet van Rensburg. You old dog. Who would have thought it?"

We spent a happy half-hour after the meeting catching up on old times. The industry is so small that you can run but you can't hide.

Chapter 36: Yardsticks

'If you can make one heap of all your winnings
And risk it on one turn of pitch-and-toss,
And lose, and start again at your beginnings
And never breathe a word about your loss.' – Rudyard
Kipling

Louis and I had co-opted a metallurgist, Stan Blockwood, and an accountant, Taktotha Hullum, onto the board. Apart from being excellent in their functional capacities, they also had to pass the 'great fun to hang out with' test, which they did with flying colours. I need to preface this chapter with a warning: please move on to the next chapter if you are easily, or even less easily, offended...

In my experience, the use of the word 'cunt' is reserved for the most offensive people... and for your closest (male) friends. There's a curious circularity to British humour that means that the worst insults are also terms of endearment, with only context able to help outsiders to tell the difference. I therefore feel very comfortable saying to my best mates, "How you going, you old cunt?" They might take offence, but only about being called old.

We had taken our new board members to check out the mine. One of the directors of the seller was arrogant, racist and completely full of himself, with all the character traits of a snide gutter rat – in short, a twat. Having highlighted his best qualities, I leave it to you to now imagine his worst. Stan came up with the cuntology scale, on which you measure the level of cuntiness of all the twats in your life. It starts with the best of them, a half-cunt, has no functional use, and half the size of a regular cunt, so still a cunt, and goes right up to Taktotha's contribution of the elephantine cunt… a cunt of epic proportions, trumpeting away loudly while stamping on anything that gets in the way. Clearly, Stan and Taktotha were men of the highest levels of perception and thus fully qualified to be board members of a mining company. Their wisdom exceeded their beauty.

We went into overdrive to try to raise the money for the purchase and refurbishment of the mine. I had managed to get a presentation slot and a booth at the Mines and Money conference in London. We printed posters, business cards, presentation copies and other giveaways in a wide assortment of colours. I had a speaking slot on the first morning and had practiced my speech a couple of dozen times. Unusually for me, I had it word-perfect.

Our lawyers called me that evening. You can't mention either Village or Cons Murch, they said. Village hadn't made a press release on the exclusivity agreement and it would cause a massive problem for them with the Johannesburg Stock Exchange regulators.

"You're bloody kidding me," I exclaimed. "You can't do this to us. I am on in ten hours and I have to go out to dinner, get drunk and sleep."

Louis and I came up with a cunning plan. I changed all references to 'Cons Murch' to 'Project X'. This had the most amazing effect. Usually after a presentation, you might get three or four people at the booth asking questions and trying to get to know you. This time we were four rows deep in mining folk, all wanting a clue as to what Project X was. It worked brilliantly – we received a shedload of interest, all quite by accident.

We obtained promises for the required funds, subject to diligence. Our brokers, having achieved the target, slacked off and stopped pushing for more. This proved to be a colossal mistake, since our main backer decided to pull out at the fifty-ninth minute of the eleventh hour. I would have bet the farm on him staying in, but someone had whispered in his ear that gold was headed down to 500 bucks an ounce and he was spooked.

Unfortunately, we were not able to attract the funding we needed to press ahead in the remaining hours of the exclusivity period, and we were surprised when Village wouldn't extend. At first, we thought they had secretly attained another interested party, but this was uncharitable on our part; they had simply run out of money and put the company into Business Rescue, a form of debtor-led insolvency.

We were swimming now in a sea of sharks, all smelling blood and looking to pick up an asset dirt-cheap and asset-strip what was left. We managed to find backers for this process and stayed in the race. The liquidator asked for best and final bids; we made a modest bid, with a promise of 130 million rand of capital investment and jobs for 200 people.

We were not the highest bidder, which was a major disappointment for the Stibium team. I wrote to the management team and to the unions, who had all been hoping for a rebirth with us, saying how sorry I was that we wouldn't be working together, and wishing them the best of luck with the new owners. What I didn't know was that the highest bidder didn't automatically win the tender; in fact, under South African law, the unions had the power to decide. The unions, under the guidance of my good old friend Boet, decided to reject the highest bidder, and we were back in the game. For a short time, Louis and I had control of ten percent of the world's known antimony resources, but the greedy investors quickly diluted us down to ten percent of that for their $15 million capital input.

We renamed the mine Stibium Mopani, after the Mopani tree prevalent in the locality. The Mopani tree is an extremely hard wood tree whose leaves feed the Mopani worm, a source of protein; being both hardy and a food source were images we wanted to cultivate. Over the next three years we restarted operations and created jobs for 370 people. Within twelve months we were at break-even and moved into profitability. Of course, we faced a number of challenges, chief among which were the poor rains which meant we were woefully short of water for processing. However, the top management team gelled well, and the workforce were well disposed towards us.

My abiding memories of this time revolve around the wildlife. Living in the deep Limpopo there was plenty of it. At one stage, I was sitting on Boet's stoop, chewing the fat about how to solve various mine issues, when his dog started barking at me. I thought for a second that he'd got rabies and was going to bite a chunk out of my calf muscle, which he had been eyeing with salivating intent. I looked down just as the head of a black mamba slithered into view below the chair I had been hitherto slumped in. Usain Bolt had nothing on me that evening. I was on the table bleating like a sacrificial lamb in a nanosecond. Boet, used to these things, was crying with laughter.

I must be attractive to these snakes. A few weeks later I was having a late breakfast with a certain Bruce, just in from Australia, at the Sellati Lodge Hotel. I looked up to see Lorinda, the buxom front-of-house lady, brandishing a broom above her head and then pummelling a rather large fellow who had slithered through the door. The kitchen staff disappeared faster than fat kids chasing an ice-cream van. Having battered the six-footer to death, Lorinda turned around and calmly asked us if we wanted coffee, as if nothing had happened.

"You don't have something stronger, do you?" asked the rather stunned Bruce. In the absence of kitchen staff, we made do with brandy and toast.

We also had a great relationship with the local farmers. I am certain that they were making far more money than us breeding sable and other rare species. One had a massive crash of rhinos - feeding them was a most inspiring sight. Keeping poachers away from the wildlife was a constant battle for them. We helped, pooling our security capabilities to try to prevent the poaching. I remember one day, when I was out looking into some old adit (a tunnel that goes into the side of a hill) with the head of security, we spotted leopard paw-prints at the muddy entrance. I sent the security man ahead: after all, he had the gun. We got a little further in and then spotted the smaller prints of leopard cubs. Security was getting visibly nervous. I began to metaphorically shit myself.

We went another hundred metres. I heard a low growl ahead and we turned tail and took off for the entrance, emerging like buttered bullets. Probably the wrong approach, but I reasoned that, as long as I was faster than Mr. Security, I had at least a modest chance of seeing tomorrow.

Whilst I was enjoying this job immensely, the long commute to South Africa was starting to play havoc with my relationships at home. My wife and kids had come to visit a couple of times, but the long periods in between, and the twenty-six hours of travelling to get home, became wearing. After three years, I received an attractive offer to join a minerals group in Macedonia in a full time role. I had been advising them from a distance over the years, and given the Stibium investor was slowly diluting my ownership interest to bugger all, I decided to move on. Clearly, I hadn't learned my lesson from Popka about doing detailed due diligence on my new company. Big mistake.

Chapter 37: Odds and Sods

"There may be no 'I' in team, but there are three in narcissistic." – Jack Shaft

Based on the Greek myth of Narcissus, we refer to someone as a narcissist when they are vain and self-centred, and certainly not if they smell of flowers. But narcissism goes well beyond that. Narcissists have an exaggerated sense of self-importance, a constant need for attention and praise, and an overwhelming sense of entitlement. They typically lack empathy and indulge in power fantasies. It is close to impossible for them to confess to a mistake. Above all, they have a habit of exploiting others for personal gain. All great characteristics for stuffing up any leadership role, whether it be running the most powerful nation on earth, running a tiger sanctuary, or, running a resource-focused company with neither experience nor qualifications.

How I ended up with these clowns still surprises me to this day. I had been asked by a Kosovar friend who had a light association with them, if I would be interested in joining Sun Resources Group, a private company based in Macedonia, as a non-executive director in order to bring some industry experience to the board. My main role was to read board papers, turn up to board meetings to discuss them and offer guidance. To be frank, I didn't really want to join the company; at the first board meeting, after I had endured listening to the other board members talk absolute twaddle about mining and exploration projects for over half an hour, the Chairman asked for my opinion I gave it to him straight.

"One thing that's absolutely clear to me is that everyone around this table knows absolutely fuck-all about mining or natural resources." I thought that ought to get me off the hook.

Unfortunately, they found the truth refreshing. My blunt synopsis and cynicism didn't have my desired outcome. Consequently, every three months, I would turn up and say something equally forthright and critical only to be applauded for my candour each time. I couldn't shake them.

My sense of the management and the other board members was as a bunch of nice guys who at least had a sense of brotherly camaraderie in that boys' club, back slapping, "we're all in this together" sort of way. I performed this non-executive role for three years whilst working as CEO of the Stibium group and I would like to think that I offered some good advice. Despite their promises to do so, they had not paid me anything for my inputs. Sun Resources never made it into profit but managed to limp on with the help of investor capital. Becoming profitable was a mirage that was always another four weeks away.

Sunny had managed to snag the son of a billionaire packaging magnate from North America as an investor and business partner. The investor was of the view that his 'we're all real men together, mister nice guy, don't worry Daddy will pay' attitude was what kept everything running smoothly. Sun fawned on him as he did with all his investors until the money tap was closed off. Daddy was smart enough to keep a tight rein on his son so the amount of wasted money being ploughed into to Sunny's next ill-advised project was at least limited to single digit millions. Sunny was profligate whenever he did bring money into the company, spending it on flashy cars or big promotional events involving minor British royals. I did get the opportunity at one of his dinners to sit next to 'His Royal Highness'. To be fair, HRH probably knew more about the mining business than Sunny Boy – but that was a low bar.

At this time, I was keen to move on from Stibium so when these guys invited me to join the company as COO for the main group, I fell for the, "Hail fellow, you're so lucky to have met me, because we need you right now," charade. Everyone is susceptible to flattery.

It didn't take long for Sun White, the CEO of the main company, to show his true colours. I guess I should have spotted it before because anybody who chooses their company name from the other end of the spectrum from SMIIBAW is showing all the signs. Please shoot me if you ever see Jack's Gold Company, or Shaft's Apple of the Earth Mining.

Sun lived his life in the belief that great things were just about to happen to him simply because he was so special by virtue of being himself. And for a while, I was a believer too, falling for his massive self-confidence which with hindsight I can now see was mere arrogance. I turned a blind eye to it though, driven by a need to try to save my marriage by having my family with me, and a belief that I would be able to instil a technical and professional ethic into the company. I rapidly discovered he was 'fake it till you make it' pumped up on steroids, fancying himself as Elon Musk, Steve Jobs and Mark Zuckerberg all rolled into one, as he strutted around the place emulating their less savoury characteristics by practicing being a jerk. I lost count of the number of times he told me that, "In just another four weeks we are going to hit the jackpot and we will all be rich and never have to work again," or, "This is already a two billion dollar company, just as soon as the world recognises the power of the technology we are developing." All this despite the fact that staff hadn't been paid for half a year. He'd set completely unrealistic and unnecessary deadlines, driving his employees to work extremely long hours, on pointless tasks.

My instincts screamed out to me to get away from this guy, but my other needs drove me on. The door back to Stibium was firmly closed as, after I had resigned, they had quickly found a replacement. I convinced myself that I would be able to make the zinc project work successfully and get out before Sun, once again, managed to snatch defeat from the jaws of victory.

His past was littered with people he had used and cast aside. I think the chances of him sharing the spoils, should one of his hair-brained schemes actually work, were non-existent. I often heard him disparaging his most senior people, as I have no doubt he did me. Yes, he could be amiable and charming particularly to strangers or those with money. But in reality it was always just a charade. As long as you ascribed to the 'Sun White Is a Genius Club' and stroked his insatiable ego, you would be tolerated. Now I've finished being nice about him, I will tell you what I really think.

Sun White, of course, had a feeble sense of humour. He had the maturity of a pubescent boy. If it didn't pertain to genitals, the expulsion of gas (or the simulation of such hand-in-armpit style), or YouTube skateboarding fails, it was beyond him. He was not one to take expert advice and he constantly suffered from the Not Invented Here Syndrome. For example, we needed an industrial-sized, atmospherically controlled, furnace for extracting esoteric metals from salts. With furnace geometry, the best shape is a cylinder. That's in fact one reason why soft drink cans are cylindrical because it is the best shape to handle pressure. Sun White's furnaces were cubes, because cylinders are difficult to make, and if you only employ a bunch of blokes with stick welders that's all you can get. He was also terribly paranoid, refusing to involve a third party to manufacture cylindrical furnaces because they might steal his design.

For about three months, I tried to run the main company's operations as COO. Each day, we had short morning meetings to set priorities; we conducted safety talks and risk assessments, and developed risk registers and comprehensive reporting systems; all the things that proper companies do. This was all the more important given that our company was processing tantalum using large quantities of hydrogen fluoride. The fumes from hydrogen fluoride, even at low levels, can irritate the eyes, nose and respiratory tract. Breathing it in at high levels can cause death from irregular heartbeats or from fluid build-up in the lungs. A small splash of high-concentration hydrogen fluoride products on the skin can be fatal. So mildly risky then. How Sunny Boy had managed to obtain his environmental and operational permits in days and not years is a shrouded secret. That, combined of course with ineptitude on the part of the permitting agency, who to be fair, would have had no experience of such hazardous materials.

Sunny would attend my daily safety meetings for about five minutes and when he wasn't centre of attention, he would leave. Eventually, he instructed me to stop having the meetings on the basis that it was a waste of working time. I started having safety meetings on the jobs first thing each morning with each of my staff at their workplaces, effectively doing an early morning round. It was sub-optimal because you couldn't get different viewpoints from the team on specific safety issues, how an issue might affect their element of the work, and of course getting the input on each risk from a diverse and experienced team.

On one occasion the Serbian Minister of the Interior visited the plant. It was the day after a new solvent extraction pipe had been fitted and the guys were testing it. This was Sunny's pet project and I had not been allowed to be involved in the design or operating procedures. Sunny of course considered this project as super special, and he thus kept it super-secret. The fact that other, far more easily maintained, safer and efficient systems were used elsewhere in the world did not matter to him. He went to great lengths to conceal the design from what he truly believed was industrial espionage. Indeed, he made all of us call different items of equipment or processes by women's names rather than their proper names, so that if anyone heard employees talking about some work-related topic, they wouldn't understand what was being said.

"Mary is not behaving very well; I think she needs a more vigorous stirring."

"KISS on Kate, she can become very complex."

"Sharron needs a bigger pump, if we're going to get a pregnant solution."

It was puerile stuff. In any event, any rival company listening in to Sun Resources Group would have known instantly what was being discussed simply from the context. Further, they would have wet themselves laughing at the stupidity of it all.

Anyway, the Serbian minister was being shown around when, all of a sudden, the end blew off of Sun's new solvent extraction pipe, and what could have been hydrogen-fluoride-loaded fluid started pissing all over the plant, the pumps working ever faster as resistance to the fluid pressure dropped. Plumes of spray erupted geyser like into the air. I screamed at the minister to run, then grabbed him by the collar and bundled him out the back door before sending him off for a long, cold safety shower. It wasn't our finest hour. It was at this moment that I resolved to extricate myself from my role as Chief Operating Officer at Sun Resources Group as quickly as possible.

Fortunately, the opportunity arose a couple of weeks later when I was asked to spearhead, as CEO, a listed company into which Sun was backing some zinc assets. Since Sun Resources would also be providing services to the new company, I would have been conflicted as COO, so I seized the opportunity to resign all my roles and involvement in Sun's company. I couldn't escape him completely, but at least I would not end up holding responsibility for his stunts. I truly hope, for the good of the people working in the Sun, that luck continues to charm their lives.

Chapter 38: Leggedco CEO

'Out of the frying pan into the fire' – Ancient Proverb

I joined Leggedco just as Sunny Boy had persuaded its Chairman, Joli Goldstein, to issue 50 percent of the outstanding stock in order to attain the rights to a zinc oxide containing pile of dirt languishing in a ploughed field in the Balkans. So, while nominally I had escaped from Sunny boy, his company owned half the company I was to lead, and soon enough Joli invited him onto the LeggedCo board.

Joli was a self-made multimillionaire who had made his fortune doing astute deals in mining royalties and by selling companies and projects just at the right time. I liked him. He was shrewd, with a cracking dry sense of humour. When he fired me about a year later, we had a great meal together and enjoyed a chinwag about the fun and games he was about to face, having decided to assume the roles of both CEO and President of Leggedco. I always found him straightforward and pragmatic and, since I had engineered my own demise, there were no bad feelings. He had no idea what he was letting himself in for....

I started my new role with endeavour and enthusiasm. I set about building a local team of quality people while Sun tried to offload the flotsam and jetsam of his staff onto me - the people he had taken on over the years because he thought their hair colour complemented his jacket or their

243

sycophantic disposition complemented his tiny, paranoid mind.

Second-rate people commonly hire third-rate people to make themselves look like first-rate people. Sun wanted me to take his third-raters and he was upset when I point-blank refused. Regardless, he executed the transfers as soon as I was out the door and before Joli understood what was going on.

During my one-year tenure running Leggedco, I focused on building the demonstration plant whilst dodging Sunny's bullets. The plant build was made doubly difficult because Sunny Boy kept 'borrowing' essential items of equipment and then breaking them as he tried to use them for something for which they were so clearly not designed. It would have been amusing to watch from the side-lines.

We managed, against the odds, to build a functional one tonne per day demonstration plant. As we started gearing up to build a full-scale plant, I faced the challenge of Sunny Boy and his merry band of lightweights wanting the commission to design and build that new plant. As Einstein wryly noted, the difference between genius and idiocy is that there is no limit to the latter. Sunny was convinced he could do it cheaper and better than the highly-trained and experienced professionals that I had in mind.

"They're just stuck in the box way of thinking," he would intone, "Dinosaurs – they have no idea about new tech." He and Joli spent hours in discussion every day as Sunny did his utmost to torpedo my plans. I brought as many subcontracted professionals and service companies into the design team as I could, but he would constantly go behind my back direct to Joli, undermining any professionalism I had managed to build into the project. In essence, he put sticks in the spokes of my wheels at every opportunity. Within a relatively short period of time, it became clear to me that we would have to completely disengage from the Sun Resources Group. The email below, except for the name changes, is a copy of what I sent to Joli.

Dear Joli,

The following email concerns plant design but touches on larger ramifications concerning the Sun Resources Group Services contract. It is my intention, funding permitting, to bring back the professional design team I proposed for the project so that we can create a proper design layout for the new plant. I am less than convinced that the Sun team have the capability to do this. Yesterday, Sun stormed out of a meeting to discuss plant layout when I merely questioned him on the basis of the - in my opinion - poor design they are touting. Putting aside his childish tantrum (I am getting used to that now), we need to do this properly and therefore I find no other solution but to bring back the core team to get the design properly put to bed.

I would add to that there is no design concept material from the Sun Resources Group, and Sun has also made the somewhat bold statement that the original professional design work is without merit (I am paraphrasing). This clearly isn't true, and merely confirms to me that he doesn't know what he is talking about.

It has become increasingly clear to me that the Sun Resources team have other - and more pressing - agendas and don't really understand zinc processes or requirements. I have indicated to you previously that I felt our best strategy was to disengage expeditiously. Deliverable deadlines on the service contract have come and gone and, despite my numerous requests, I have yet to see a single monthly report. Clearly, they do not have the desire, the skills or the capacity necessary to fulfil this contract and we have no choice but to terminate the main contract for non-performance. Further, while there are individual pockets of capability, in every single case, these skills are continuously redirected to 'more important' work. We would be better placed to hire our own dedicated people. The only things we need from Sun Resources Group are the following fairly simple deliverables:

1) The Temporary Environmental Permit for the zinc plant needs to be assigned to our site, not theirs.

2) The input material contracts – promises of 50,000 tonnes per annum – need to be concluded and assigned to us. I am still waiting to see a single contract.

3) Possibly help with financing, though I personally don't believe they have any capability in this area given that his main investor is starting to realise that his cash is travelling down a one way street.

Furthermore, I have seen nothing of the Trafigura off-take option promised, and the financial model put together by Sun is weak and, to my mind, flawed. Our model developed by financial experts is superior, but now he has started circulating his own, there are multiple versions of the truth doing the rounds of potential investors.

Everything else they purport to be able to do would be better done by experienced professionals. I accept they could add value in plant construction, but I don't see these skills as irreplaceable in any way.

I have suggested to you that a rapid planned disengagement of Leggedco from the Sun Group as the way forward. Of course, there is another option available, which is to ask the Sun Resources Group to deliver everything. Given that they have singularly failed to deliver anything at all to time or budget, the best half of their ideas and approaches are 'Heath Robinson', and the other half are at best abjectly stupid, or worse, potentially fatally dangerous. They have virtually no background in large-scale metallurgy on their Leggedco project delivery team, and therefore planning to have them design, build and commission our plant is somewhat high risk, and I would strongly recommend against it. Indeed, if this is the approach you wish to adopt, then you had better find a new man on the ground to lead this project implementation, given the abject failure I foresee.

Yours sincerely, Jack

As you can imagine, the email caused some ripples particularly in light of the fact that Sun Resources shareholders owned 50 percent of the equity in Leggedco, and they were the incumbent service provider. It was indeed a job suicide note, and I knew it. This email resulted in Joli flying halfway across the globe for a heart-to-heart discussion, during which we decided that for me to continue would only exacerbate an already ridiculous situation. Having worked in Afghanistan, Kyrgyzstan, Kosovo, the far east of Russia and in various other challenging spots, my time with Leggedco was as close to my worst nightmare as I can recall.

I had essentially given Joli two choices: back me and do it professionally, or back Sunny Boy, and enjoy a sphincter-clenching ride on a roller coaster of stupidity. Of course, Joli had to let me go. For me, this wasn't at all like the Magadan experience. Sunny clearly thought that the sun did shine where the sun don't shine, and I was more than happy to be out of there.

Sunny, of course, put it about in the company that he had fired me, even though it was Joli, because I favoured contracting my friends and that he had to stop me; a little galling, but as with many of these stories spread by the 'winner', he'd fabricated his own version of history. Leggedco's stock market value has gradually fallen to about 3 percent of its valuation at my departure, and that is all the truth you really need.

I had in fact jumped from one role in South Africa which I loved but which was causing enormous personal strife at home in France, into a new vipers pit which was as fascinating as it was horrifying. My instincts should have told me that Sunny was an arsehole before I set off on this path. So why did I continue to go down the road once it became apparent that I was on a ship of fools? Was it technical pride that no one else could operate in the Balkans and do this better than me, or a belief that I'd be in and out and make money before Sunny wrecked the joint? Why did others continue to back him? Stupid is as stupid does, I would say, because if you keep reaching into the toilet bowl, you keep winding up with turds. I departed the field with a promise to myself: trust my instincts in future, get out as soon as you know beyond reasonable doubt that the path you are on is the wrong one. I strongly advocate to never work with people you don't respect or like – life's too short.

As a footnote on Sunny Boy, his companies still don't make any money, the people are many months behind in receiving their salaries and, I hear, he is still promising the nirvana of billions of dollars... just around another corner of hard graft for another four weeks.

Chapter 39: The Final Chapter

"Mirrors don't lie and lucky for me, they don't laugh either."
– Unknown

So, I had made it to the top of my game as CEO of a listed mining company. I gave it a good shot but with psychopaths and narcissists in the upper echelons, it was hard to step round the minefields, and I retired from the field of play. CEOs are not all bad; indeed, most are good people who really do care about their employees, the environment and local society.

I do occasionally take some consulting roles. For example, I recently worked for the Agency of Natural Resources in Georgia (the country, not the US state) assisting with their promotional efforts and the development of their mining regulations. A short note on Georgia – it is one of the most hospitable places I have ever visited. The people are incredibly friendly and helpful. As an example, one weekend whilst I was beavering away on a presentation in my hotel room, a geological professor with whom I was working called me up at two in the afternoon.

"Would you like to join my wife and I for dinner?" he enquired.

"I'd be delighted," I responded.

"Great," he said. "We'll pick you up in 15 minutes."

I showered and dressed at the double, wondering about such an early dinner date. I got to the pickup point just in time. We drove down to a riverside restaurant in Tbilisi and checked our coats in at the foyer. Diner after diner started to arrive and the professor greeted each like a long-lost brother. Wow, I thought, he knows everyone in the city. After about 15 minutes, I began to reach the conclusion that this was no ordinary dinner. As we entered the main room, I noted that the restaurant had been set up for 500 people, and a gala feast was in view. At two am the next morning, as one of the first to leave, I crawled out. I had experienced the most amazing feast, toasting for every possible purpose, and dancing lunatics with razor-sharp swords in their mouths as a celebration for this sixty-year-old professor I had only just met. I had been subsumed into the Georgian family like a puppy at a three-year-old's birthday party and we had metaphorically gorged on cake until we wanted no more. This was just one of many such welcoming experiences.

Georgians have good reason to claim they invented mining, when you consider that the Golden Fleece story originated in the country. They have an even better claim on being the birthplace of wine. Mining and wining. You can understand why it's easy for me to feel a connection to the place. Georgians know their priorities in life - I was heartened to read on a wine label:

ICEWINE is served very cold and can be paired with fruit and sweets, or enjoyed on its own as an aperitif, at the end of a meal, during the day, or even before breakfast.

It's easy to see how wine became a metaphor for so many things, from divine blood to the colour of the sea, and why it plays such an important part in this gracious culture. On one visit to the country, I read an article in the English-language weekly paper entitled "10 wines to try before you die." I was intrigued and mentioned it to my local work colleagues. On my next trip out, they presented me with the boxed sets. Something had been lost in translation though... the packaging read: "10 wines to try until you die" and indeed we did our best.

On that note, allow me to make a toast to all those hardy souls who toil in the mines, digging value from the bowels of the earth:

> May the roof above your head never fall in,
> And the people below it never fall out,
> So, raise a toast,
> To those we love most,
> For a long life, and a merry one,
> A quick death, and an easy one,
> A pretty girl, and an honest one,
> A cold beer, and another one.

Gluckauf!

(Gluckauf! Is a German miners' toast that means literally 'luck above you', Gunster assures me... It probably means 'fuck off' then!)

There are countless people who work in the mining industry. Yet whenever I meet one, we always seem to know someone in common. It's a small world and yet one on which we all rely. Just about everything we have was dependent at some stage on miners. Houses, cars, phones, laptops. All the material once started out in the ground, before being wrestled from their resting place by a person wearing a hard hat and sporting a large shovel.

I have now retreated to a rural idyll in the Pyrenees and am deeply engaged in building an English pub. What could possibly go wrong? I still have a strong hankering to prove that I can successfully run a small mining company, given the partial successes so far. Hopefully, I won't upset too many people with this tome, and that dream will one day happen. I hope, if you have read this far, that you have found some amusement in these tales from the tunnels.

And so our journey ends. When I started writing it, I jotted down a few anecdotes and quickly reached 5,000 words (four chapters or so) and then stopped. Those were the obvious stories, but I surprised myself that the less obvious ones had more mileage in them, and I got a second wind. I found it important to approach writing like a job, and to start precisely at nine in the morning and write until lunchtime without interruption. It is said that 80 percent of people believe they have a book in them, but far less than 1 percent sit down to write, and even fewer complete the task. Why not try it? It's been cathartic for me, and hopefully, given that you have reached this point, entertaining for you.

Keep well, keep safe, enjoy your time. For time is all we have. It's been a blast. To finish this book, I leave you with one final, to my mind brilliant quote from Hunter S. Thompson:

Life should not be a journey to the grave with the intention of arriving safely in a pretty and well preserved body, but rather to skid in broadside in a cloud of smoke, thoroughly used up, totally worn out, and loudly proclaiming WOW!"

Epilogue

No doubt there are more adventures waiting around the corner. In the meantime, I am applying myself to building a pub, whilst writing a different take on this life of mine... the interesting and contradictory relationships between two people and their commitment to living which each other. You will have noticed that I have predominantly kept away from my love life in this book. I am working up the idea of a book that explores the tensions, conflicts, joys and funny things that happen when two people collide and decide to be in a relationship. The tentative title is:

"Bonkers"
By
Jack Shaft

If you enjoyed this book, then please take the time to sign up for advanced notice of my next book, and I promise to keep you informed of its progress and launch date. Please send me an email at:

Jackoshaft@gmail.com

I look forward to hearing from you. Jack